The Times of My Life

The Times of My Life

by
Jim Langford

THE TIMES OF MY LIFE

Copyright © 2015 by Jim Langford

Cover art by Sandra L. Hart

10 9 8 7 6 5 4 3 2

ISBN 978-0-9961362-3-5

Published by
CORBY BOOKS
P.O. Box 93
Notre Dame, IN 46556
www.corbypublishing.com

Manufactued in the United States of America

DEDICATION

To the family God so kindly let me be part of
To the friends whose kindness is forever with me
To the three Notre Dame Presidents:
Father Ted Hesburgh, CSC
Father Monk Malloy, CSC
Father John Jenkins, CSC
Who took a very good University
and made it into a great University
To the children volunteers and supporters who made
There Are Children Here
A sacred place

Acknowledgments

Writing a memoir, I discovered, is not easy work. Many people helped with memories and reminders, and others with critiques and cautions; the story is mine and so is the telling of it. To any who feel slighted in any way, I apologize.

I owe abundant gratitude to my wonderful Nimbi, also a writer, to Jeremy, Josh Jill, to Tim Carroll of Corby Books; Kevin Gibley, Colleen Jones and the late Sue Shidler, all of the Hammes Notre Dame Bookstore for their encouragement and support. Thanks also to Kerry Temple and Carol Schaal of Notre Dame Magazine and to Fr. Nicholas Ayo, CSC, who has been a strong supporter of our efforts and a good friend as well. Thank you to Sandra L. Hart for the art gracing the cover of this book and to Eileen Carroll for the careful editing.

To all of my friends, those who shared this ride with me and those whose gift was encouragement, my gratitude is boundless.

Preface

This book is simply an account of one man's search for purpose and happiness. No one has a life story identical to anyone else's. But there are some things we all share: challenges and efforts, hopes and disappointments, successes and failures. As I near the end of my life, I offer my story with its many twists and turns because it clearly embodies evidence of Divine Providence leading to events and opportunities that we can either embrace or eschew. Things don't just happen to us by chance and circumstance. But neither are they predetermined. We make our choices and live with their consequences.

The goal is happiness and the secret is choosing the right path to find and secure it. The imposters are powerful and most of us have to find that out for ourselves. My story is one of growing up, of seeking and finally finding the wellspring of happiness.

Books by Jim Langford

Galileo, Science and the Church

The Game is Never Over

Runs, Hits and Errors

The Cub Fan's Guide to Life

The Cub Fan's Little Book of Wisdom

Rookie (with Jerome Walton)

The Cub Fan's Book of Days

Happy Are They/Living the Beatitudes in America

Walking with God in a Fragile World

The Spirit of Notre Dame

Quotable Notre Dame

Table of Contents

—1—

Don't Hold Me Back

June 12, 1937 is a day about which I remember nothing and, at the same time, a day I will never forget. Something happened that marked me for life. Someone at St. Joseph Hospital, South Bend, Indiana, tried to stop me from being born, to hold me back from entering the world. It was a nurse. She acted out of custom and fear. In those days, nurses didn't act on their own no matter the circumstance. The doctor performed all of the important procedures. He was not there as I began crowning. He was "on his way." And so was I. The nurse placed her hand on my emerging head and held me back. Finally the doctor arrived and I was allowed to come out and take my first breath. For all intents and purposes, I'm sure it seemed like a routine birth. It wasn't.

I am not a subscriber to the psychological theory that the unfolding of one's life is determined, or at least directed, by the events of infancy. In my case, though, perhaps that theory carries at least a grain of truth.

I was nearly eighteen months old before my parents could tell for sure that something was wrong. I could barely walk. My entire left side seemed to be on a different schedule than my right side. My left leg and foot attempted steps that all too often ended in stubbed toes or a fall. My left arm was smaller and less agile than my right.

My parents took me to the doctor and he offered the startling diagnosis that I had spina bifida and I would likely not live more than a few years. Wise enough to seek a second opinion, they took me to the University of Michigan Hospital in Ann Arbor. It did not take the specialists there long to figure out what had happened. The nurse's pressure on my head had caused me to have a stroke. They said my body needed to grow and develop before physical therapy would be helpful. In the meantime as I was growing, I should be made to exercise as much as possible.

I don't think I noticed or dwelt much on my differences until kindergarten when the other kids began to ask me, "What's wrong with your leg? Why do you walk funny?" My parents consoled me with the promise that, as I grew and with plenty of exercise, some day those questions would stop.

Happily, luckily, I was born into an extraordinary family. My dad was raised in McAllen, Texas, in the

Rio Grande Valley. He was one of three children; his brother, James, died at age 17 from acute appendicitis, and his sister eventually became a nun. Dad's father was a state bank examiner and the son of a county sheriff. His mother, Ethel, was an elegant lady, much admired in McAllen. She died of cancer a few years after my dad graduated from college. Although dad had deep and strong emotions, he seldom showed them. Gary Cooper could have taken lessons from him.

The Langfords were Episcopalians until Ethel converted to Roman Catholicism. The story is part of family history. Ethel was the daughter of Thomas Lyons McCarty, an Irish Catholic who spent four years in General Hood's Texas Brigade during the Civil War. Hood's Brigade was attached to General Robert E. Lee's special troops; T.L.'s diaries of fighting in nearly every one of Lee's battles are still in the family. He was a stubborn, prideful man. He was at Appomattox for Lee's surrender and when the Yankees offered him a horse for the trip back to Texas; he turned it down and said he'd rather walk than accept anything from a Yankee.

T.L. had been a Roman Catholic until, having paid pew rental for a year, one Sunday he found somebody in his pew. He left the building and he left the Church and became an Episcopalian. His daughter Ethel converted to Catholicism and wanted her son to go to a Catholic college. She had heard good things about Notre Dame up north and it was decided that he would enroll there in the fall of 1926. He loved being at Notre Dame. In his junior year, he converted to Roman Catholicism and was baptized by Father John O'Hara, later President of Notre Dame and eventually Cardinal of Philadelphia.

Dad graduated in 1930 and returned to McAllen. It was not the best time to find a job; the stock market had crashed, businesses were laying off workers and banks were bracing for the worst. Thanks to his father's intervention, dad secured a position as a bank teller. Within a year he met my mother at the Catholic church in Mission, Texas. How she came to be there is itself a story that illustrates the importance of chance and circumstance, or providence, in our life.

Mom was born and raised in Kankakee, Illinois, one of six children of Louis Joubert and Christine Rouleau. They were both French by way of Quebec, Canada. Louis owned and operated drug stores in the Kankakee, Momence, Manteno area of central Illinois. The Jouberts cared a great deal about education, thus my mother achieved an uncommon goal for women of that era by earning a degree in biology from Trinity College in Washington, D.C.

When Louis developed heart disease, his doctor told him to move south and adopt a slower pace. The family moved to Mission, Texas, near McAllen. She and dad had taken circuitous routes, but here they were in Texas and, having begun dating soon after they met at the church in Mission, they fell in love. She told me once that she knew she was in love with him when he came in a black tie and a tear in his eye for their date on the day Knute Rockne was killed in a plane crash in Kansas.

Were I to try to recite the wonderfulness of my mother, it would come out as a litany, a hymn, a song. She was short, 4'11", a spirited person, completely devoted to her vocation as a wife and mother. My mother devoted her life to raising four children, keeping a wonderful home, shopping wisely, sewing clothes and cooking wonderful meals on a budget. She was elegant and hardworking at the same time. I'm hoping she will be waiting on the other side with roast beef, mashed potatoes, gravy, green beans and her patented smile. I miss her every day. She stretched the family budget so that Notre Dame students could be invited for a home-cooked meal. She cared deeply about others and she never hesitated to help anyone in need. I remember how she made sandwiches for the occasional vagabond who would come up from the railroad tracks and knock on our back door on Diamond Avenue asking for food. Word must have gotten around among the boxcar travelers that if you knocked on our door you would get food and milk. She set a wonderful example for us, so we were not surprised when she and my dad left for Chile for two years in the Peace Corps in 1961, or that at the time of her death in 1975, she and my dad were in the Dominican Republic working to help the poor.

She was proud of her husband and seemed to know and accept that she owned a large share of the credit for everything my dad achieved. Dad always wore a suit and tie to Notre Dame. Mom bought his clothes at Gilberts and Max Adler, and her care for them kept them like new for a long time.

A few weeks after their marriage, while still getting settled in McAllen, dad received a letter from Father Leonard Carrico, CSC, Dean of Faculty at Notre Dame, inviting him to consider joining the faculty for the fall semester of 1931. He would be teaching Spanish, a language he had mastered growing up on the border with Mexico. It took him no time to convince my mother to move back north.

Dad's salary was set at $2,000 a year. But he was delighted to be back at Notre Dame and, as he said, it beat working at a bank, especially when so many were failing in the Depression. They moved to South Bend and bought a small house on Corby Boulevard, close to campus.

When he reported to Notre Dame, he was assigned to an office in the main building. A few months earlier, it had been the office of Knute Rockne! There was a walk-in safe in the office containing some of Rockne's belongings. Dad helped Bonnie Rockne, Knute's widow, move those things to her home. I remember going to that office as a child and playing in the large safe. One time I discovered an unmarked package wrapped in brown paper. I opened it to find four mint copies of a book, *The Four Winners* by Knute Rockne.

Shortly after I was born in 1937, we moved to a larger home at 1245 Diamond Avenue. I was the third child, after my sister, Lois, and my brother, Walter

McCarty Langford, Jr. (which we shortened to Mac). It is a two-story, wood-framed house located near a steep embankment leading down to then oft-used railroad tracks that curved under a viaduct on Portage Avenue. Up the hill on the other side of the tracks there was a vast open space beyond which was the Drewrys Brewery. The field was used for victory gardens during World War II. When the war was over and the gardens were abandoned, the kids in the neighborhood dug forts, cleared space for a ball diamond and spent time flying kites or looking for frogs.

That field was important to me. The war was still going on when I turned seven. Every time I went to a movie, the Pathé News gave vivid updates on the Allied progress toward victory. Many of the movies were, in fact, propaganda films portraying how awful our enemies were. South Bend had blackout practices in case the Germans or Japanese came to bomb the Studebaker plant or Bendix, or other manufacturing sites in the area.

I was ever ready. By age seven I knew the shapes and sizes of all enemy aircraft and dreamed of personally capturing an enemy pilot who would crash in our field. I had goggles and a leather helmet, but no weapon except a baseball bat. The bombers never came. But the Cold War did. It was not long after World War II ended that the United States and the USSR were rattling swords at each other. When it was clear that the Soviets also had the atom bomb, schools, including Holy Cross, began instructing students how to get safely under their desks in case of attack—never mind that an A bomb would liquify everything, even desks. And people actually built and stocked bomb shelters in their back yards. Sermons were preached on whether one was morally obliged to share their bomb shelter with neighbors.

In most ways, the seasons of my youth were a miniature Garden of Eden. Summers, especially, had their own rhythms. All the neighborhood kids played together. In the late afternoons, we waited for the Studebaker and Bendix workers to drive down Diamond Avenue on their way to Portage Avenue or Angela Boulevard. Once they had passed, we could add the street to our play space. Dinner was at six, then we assembled again for a game of Kick the Can or Capture the Flag. Once dusk faded into darkness, it was time to go home for the night.

I have nothing but happy memories of Christmas on Diamond Avenue. The excitement of that morning was fueled by opening presents and fishing around the pieces of coal in my stocking, hung by the chimney with care, to find a tee shirt or two, some toys or games, a new piece for my train set, a Cubs sticker or other things. We didn't have money for the lavish or extensive haul garnered by other kids. But we knew that it wasn't about money, it was that every gift came with thoughtfulness and love.

I treasured being able to dip into my savings jar for the collection of change I had earned by running errands in the neighborhood, shoveling snow, cutting grass or sweeping porches. I would take the Portage Avenue bus downtown and shop. For mom I'd find a bracelet, a small bottle of skin conditioner, or maybe a scarf. For my dad it was Irish linen handkerchiefs, a tie, or Yardley's talc. For Lois and Mac I bought small items with whatever money was left.

Just as important as gifts, the splendor of the day was celebrated with a dinner that would be savored for a year. The feast featured turkey, French peasant dressing, mashed potatoes and gravy, cranberry sauce, and homemade pie for dessert. We always had guests with us: perhaps students from far away, or a newly appointed faculty member with his family. It was that way on Thanksgiving too and many times during the academic year. Notre Dame students knew the Langfords were always ready to host them.

I even remember the Christmas I lost my belief in Santa Claus, only to have it restored by a clever trick dad pulled. Getting ready to leave for Midnight Mass he loaded us in the car and then suddenly remembered that he needed to stoke the coal-burning furnace before we left. He said he'd be right back. He returned and we left for church. When we got home it was clear Santa had been there. The stockings were filled, more gifts were under the tree and the cookies we had left for Santa were gone. How could I have doubted?

What I wouldn't give to have a replay of that time. My heart and feelings are still fed by those memories.

I also can picture the blue 1938 Plymouth four-door sedan that was our car before and during World War II.

That car lasted a long time, but not much longer than the War. On the day the Japanese surrendered, dad piled us all in the car and headed downtown to join the spontaneous stream of celebrators who converged there. In the middle of a long line of cars, drivers honking and waving, our Plymouth quit. Just like that.

Back then, people didn't just sit there and honk to show irritation. Several men got out of their cars, pushed us to the side of the street and offered to look at the motor or give us some gas.

I don't remember how, only that we got home that afternoon. That car lasted until 1946 when we got a new Plymouth. Dad developed a habit after that of trading in for a new one every two years or so. The only one I cared about was the 1952 Plymouth two-tone (crimson and gray)—that was the car in which I learned to drive in 1953.

I cannot leave reminiscing about my years growing up without a salute to one of my loves. Some of us, those who loved baseball, built a diamond in the field east of Drewrys. Kids came from neighboring areas to play with or against us. And we each had our own identity. I was Bob Rush, Andy Pafko or Hank Sauer. I was always the last one chosen by the captains. But it didn't matter. I just wanted to play, to belong.

Baseball was an important part of my life, then and since. My favorite team, since the age of 11, has been the Chicago Cubs. I read books about the Cubs, studied box scores daily and ran home from school so I could hear the last few innings via Bert Wilson on

WIND Chicago. We didn't have a TV, but radio played to the imagination and it was more than enough. All too often, the Cubs would be trailing in the late innings, but Bert reminded us that "The game is never over 'til the last man is out." I believed him. He made me an optimist. I would not trade those hours sitting by the radio listening to my Cubs for anything.

The walk to Holy Cross Grade School was four blocks from our house. Because I walked slowly, Lois and Mac had to stand and wait for me to catch up with them about every block. I was bullied at recess and after school. I was fair game for several kids who regularly razed me and called me "Limpy Langford" and "Gator Arm." Sometimes they pushed me around. More often, they simply jeered and laughed. Their words and laughs were like darts that stung me in my spirit.

Sometimes when I had been stung enough, my anger led me to strike out at my tormentors. That always attracted a crowd of onlookers who wanted to witness a fight, but not to be in one. Most of the time I lost. My smallness and lack of coordination made me too slow to avoid punches or to land some of my own. The names and taunts hurt me more than the hits. It is hard to feel good about yourself when some of your peers insist on ridiculing you for something you can't help.

I have never told anyone what I am about to write.

In the mornings at Holy Cross School, we were marched into the church to attend Mass every morning. The nuns taught us religion as well as they could, but it was more devotional than doctrinal. We practically had to memorize the Baltimore Catechism. We learned that God loves each and every one of us uniquely and personally. But if that was true, why was I being targeted by the bullies?

We had learned about Guardian Angels and that everyone had one for protection and guidance. Where was mine when I needed help?

Still, I said the prayer:

> Angel of God, my guardian dear,
> to whom His love entrusts me here,
> ever this day [night] be at my side
> to light and guard, to rule and guide. Amen.

I talked a lot to my Guardian Angel, but my angel was clearly a pacifist.

I prayed hard for lots of things—for my parents and grandparents, my brother and sister—and for help to do better and be better. And I prayed to stop inventing things in confession. I did that sometimes so that the priest wouldn't be bored.

But in the recesses of my heart I also collected a daily list of schoolmates for whom I could not wish good things. I wanted God to mete out punishment to my abusers. My "hit" list often had the same names and I hoped they would be made to suffer. But it always seemed that I suffered more than they did.

I think it was in fifth grade that a girl in my class took an interest in me, smiled at me, made me feel good inside. Her name was Mary T. Dempsey and I came to like her for her goodness. She was a girl and a friend.

Then something happened. She began to miss school days, occasionally at first and then for two weeks or so. One day, the principal, Sister James Frances came into our classroom and told us that Mary T. had died. If it was God who took her instead of one of the bullies on my list, then maybe God wasn't perfect after all.

I have never forgotten Mary T. More than 60 years later I can picture her with a smile, frozen in time. I have missed her all of these years.

In sixth grade I started undergoing physical therapy twice a week. It consisted mainly of a long session in the whirlpool tub followed by a strenuous massage of the muscles behind my knee. I was able to feel those muscles loosen and stretch a bit. I will never forget the moment when I came out from a treatment and I could actually put my heal down before my toes. It felt wonderful! I looked up in time to see my mother and her good friend Lois Scannell wiping away tears.

By now I was starting to make more friends and they helped silence the bullies; by seventh grade I was popular. Classmates began to cheer for me when I went out for the school basketball and softball teams. People became interested in me and enjoyed my sense of humor. Life was better. I put many miles on the Schwinn bicycle I bought at Albrights for $32.50, using money I had earned delivering flyers from door to door for a medical insurance company. Candy bars and cokes were a nickel; gasoline was 18 cents a gallon. A dime was the going rate for running an errand for a neighbor.

I was eleven when my little sister was born. Mom

said that Liz was her "Autumn Lamb" and all of us treasured her and spoiled her without end. I learned early on that she would serve well as a "chick magnet." All I had to do was to offer to babysit, put her in my Radio Flyer Red Wagon and head over to Muessel Park. Girls my age quickly crowded around to see her.

It turned out that the four of us Langford children were actually quite different from each other. Lois, five years my senior, had many friends, and several of the boys that came around to see her were interesting, especially the one with the Cushman Motor Scooter. Lois and I got along well most of the time, though I remember one time when I aggravated her sufficiently that she lost her cool and chased me down Diamond Avenue with a broom in her hand. She was an accomplished student and won a scholarship to St. Mary's College. We were proud of her.

My brother was something of an introvert; I could not really tell what he was feeling, even when I set out to bug him.

Walter's middle name is McCarty, a tribute to a great-grandfather on our dad's side. So, instead of Walter or Walt, we always called him "Mac." He's almost four years my senior. When I was in sixth grade, he was a sophomore in high school. We did not have very many friends in common, except for kids in our neighborhood.

Even though we were very different personalities (he was always quiet and interior and I wasn't), I always looked up to him. The best example of his loyalty

I can remember happened when I was about 10 and I was flying a kite in the field across the railroad tracks from our back yard. He saw three older guys come up to me and cut the string on my kite. He and a neighbor kid ran across the tracks and took on the three bullies in a real fight. I tried to help but my kicking wasn't very accurate. I've never forgotten that day and that event. It said a lot about my brother.

A major feature of my childhood years was our biannual trips to Mexico City and beyond. It was a car trip on two-lane highways for 2,100 miles each way. Dad was working on graduate degrees at the National University of Mexico. My parents enrolled the three of us in Mexican schools for the summer. It was a lesson in what it feels like to be a minority, especially as one who does not speak the language. But it was a good way to learn about people, culture and Spanish by immersion.

In all my years I never heard either of my parents say a derogatory word about anyone because of race, nationality or creed. We are living proof that intolerance isn't genetic; it is taught to children by parents, older siblings, or classmates.

We always rented an apartment for our summers in Mexico City. While dad was at school, we often went shopping with mom at the mercado or the bakery. She could prepare a meal fit for a king on the budget of a pauper.

I learned a lot on those "vacations." I still bristle when I hear anyone call Mexicans "lazy." I saw hardworking people grinding out a living day-in and day-out.

The car rides to and from Mexico City were character-building. Try that in a 1952 Plymouth with adults in the front and three offspring in the back. As the smallest, I was always stuck in the middle. Most everyone knows what that feels like on an airplane. We did not have air conditioning. Conveniently, there were seams on the back seat dividing the space into three distinct portions.

I raised hell every time Lois or Mac encroached into my space. If the argument escalated, dad would issue a warning. If necessary, being ambidextrous, he would steer with his left hand and his right would reach over the back of his seat in search of someone to punish. Usually, it was me.

In later years Mac and I shared some great times on various trips to Mexico. And then, when he graduated from Notre Dame and became a lieutenant in the Air Force, times to see him were too few. We stayed in touch, sent each other crazy and creative gifts for birthdays (like the rubber mask of my least favorite politician, Richard Nixon, that came with birthday greetings from him in 1972).

But it was in more recent years that my brother proved that he is still protecting me and my kite. I came down with cancer about six years ago and had to have some serious surgery. Walter and his wife Barb came up from Florida and stayed a week caring for me. That mission was repeated two years later when I slipped on ice and broke my leg.

Walter is the best brother a person could have. As he reads this I know what he would tell me: "Go fly a kite!"

In terms of my physical status, much more work had to be done: more exercise, more treatment, and a new sport...tennis.

My dad had taken on more duties at Notre Dame to increase his income bit by bit. In 1940, at the urging of his friend and mentor Pedro DeLandero, he took over as head coach of the Notre Dame tennis and fencing teams. Over the next 13 years, his tennis teams won 95 and lost 30 and earned a national championship in 1944. His 13 years as fencing coach yielded a record of 155 wins and 35 losses.

At the age of 10, I had made hitting tennis balls with varsity Notre Dame players part of my regular routine. I liked the sport and learned how to compensate for my leg and arm by adjusting my feet, anticipating where the ball would be coming, and developing an unorthodox serve since my left arm couldn't toss the ball up high enough or straight enough to allow a standard serve. Dad didn't have time to coach me, but his players helped me learn the game and develop some shots. I wanted to get good at it. Dad put up boards to make a hitting wall on the back inside of the garage. I learned racket control and placement by spending countless hours hitting tennis balls off those boards, besting imaginary opponents with the persona of Jack Kramer, whose name was on my Wilson racquet.

When I was fourteen, we moved from Diamond Avenue to a bigger, nicer house, closer to Notre Dame and only a block from where St. Joseph's High School was being built. Lois was now a sophomore at

St. Mary's College and Mac was about to enroll as a freshman at Notre Dame. I missed Diamond Avenue. Decades later, in 2008, I went back to look around and recollect. I wrote in my journal:

I went back to Diamond today. By now it was no longer serene; in fact it had become a high-crime area. No kids were playing outside, or riding bikes or selling lemonade. I spotted a workman coming out of our old house. I stopped and asked whether I could look inside. He said sure. The configuration of the rooms was mostly the same, but things I had expected to recognize—the oak woodwork, the kitchen and dining room—were starkly not as I remembered them. The room my dad had built for me in the basement and where I spent nearly endless hours playing with my Lionel electric train, was gone. As I came up the stairs from the basement, I could almost picture my mother standing at the wringer washer caring for our clothes. And then I saw something I did remember; it was the rounded railing that guided all of us up and down the basement steps. I wanted to tell my host, a fireman who had bought the house to fix it into a rental property, that the railing meant something to me and I would like to buy it. But I didn't. It was enough just to know that it was still there.

The back yard was different too. The one-car wooden garage where I had spent hours and hours hitting tennis balls was gone, demolished. Had my forehand shots been that powerful? The large pussy willow bush in the back yard had vanished. I had pretended that it was the outfield fence at Wrigley Field and by throwing a tennis ball against the upper part of the house I could induce flyballs that I caught crashing the "wall."

The railroad tracks below our back yard, the same tracks that carried several trains a day back then, now stand idle. Images of children carrying schoolbooks and lunch boxes along the tracks are real now only in phantasms that sometimes bubble up from memory.

If that hill across the tracks stored echoes of children's glee—whether from sledding, riding bikes or playing ball— my voice is in there. But that place is quiet now, no longer peopled by little ones who feel safe enough to spend hours there. Places may be corrupted by time and circumstances, but memories are not.

While still living on Diamond, I started my own newspaper, *The Sport Club News*—it was about the goings on in the neighborhood (at least the good stuff). I typed it with one finger on an old Smith Corona, making as many carbon copies as I could. I sold them for a nickel. I liked thinking of myself as a writer. I never lost that aspiration.

I graduated from Holy Cross Grade School in 1951. At the ceremony, I was shocked to hear my name called as winner of a scholarship to Central Catholic High School. I would soon begin my new life as a teen in high school.

My childhood is tied to a time and place that now exists only in memory. Kids today probably don't lie down in a field and watch clouds move across the sky while letting their imagination decipher the shapes that float above them. The houses are still there, but now they shelter people who fear each other, live behind triple-locked doors, and see things with a suspicion born of prudence and common sense. Gone are the days when children and adults could easily distinguish right from wrong. Gangs back then were just kids from nearby neighborhoods up for a snowball fight or a football or baseball game. Public parks were safe places. The process of self-definition seemed less complicated than it soon became. In retrospect, there were plenty of things wrong with that time and its culture. It was racist, male dominated, and rigid. Still, had we known that those times would not last forever, we might have celebrated them more. The squeals of delight coming from kids riding their bikes along the roller-coaster-like path on the top of the hill across the tracks find no echoes now. Like most kids, I was ready to give up all of this community, all of this time-passing fun to move on to life's next stage. Young people don't stay nostalgic for long.

—2—

Freedom's Just Another Name...

I did not know what to expect in high school. Neither did just about anybody else. The whole school, all boys, counted only 167 students; there were 32 of us entering the Central Catholic freshman class. The problem was there was no place to put us. As a small, Catholic school for boys, administered and staffed by the Holy Cross Brothers, Central Catholic was housed on the second floor of St. Matthew's Grade School. It was already crowded. At the time, there were five Catholic high schools in South Bend: Central Catholic for boys; a girls school, St. Joseph Academy; and St. Mary's Academy, an exclusive boarding school for girls; St. Hedwig's; and South Bend Catholic, a Polish co-ed school on the west side.

The Brothers spent the summer searching for a place where they could accommodate us. The best they could do was to clean up and re-open a four-room, two-story, wood frame building that had formerly been a grade school belonging to St. Mary's Parish, in the middle of a German neighborhood on the southwest side of town. On the outside of the building there was a sign proclaiming "St. Marian Schule, 1884." It was a dump. But we made it our dump.

There was an advantage: it was less than two blocks to St. Joseph Academy, the all-girls high school which was lodged atop St. Patrick's Grade School. The neighborhood was mostly Blacks and elderly Germans. The city busline came from the courthouse downtown along Western Avenue to Taylor Street.

For us, the crucial factor was that we had no upperclassmen, initiations, or harassment. From day one, we ruled! We were free; we had nothing to lose by acting out and acting up. Or so we thought.

We made that old building our playground and we took no prisoners among the young Holy Cross Brothers who were sent to practice teach us. It wasn't exactly "Blackboard Jungle" but neither was it a normal school experience. The more experienced brothers on the faculty knew how to tone us down with detentions that resulted in two whacks on the seat of the pants with a broom handle for each misdeed. But the young ones were fair game. We were good at changing rows every time the teacher was writing on the board. For a true highlight, we hooked up a car firecracker to the ignition on the brothers' station wagon and when Brother Quentin turned the starter, it caused some excitement; we never tired of inventing ways to make every test an open-book test. It never occurred to us that we might be causing some of the brothers to reconsider their vocation, at least in terms of teaching in high school.

I tried out for the freshman football team. I wanted to be a quarterback because my right arm had developed well by compensating for what the left arm couldn't do. But the coach decided I wasn't big enough, fast enough or lithe enough for that position. He told me to try out for guard. Since I weighed only 125 pounds, that assignment was clearly not meant for me. I turned in my equipment.

I started going to mixers (a puzzling name since the boys stood together on one side of the room and the girls on the other). Now and then, I'd work up the courage to go over and ask a girl to dance, but it had to be to a slow song because I was never meant to jitterbug.

I developed a crush on a girl named Suzy and we agreed to meet every morning in front of the courthouse and walk together to our schools, only a block or so apart. Our time on the phone was limited by the fact that her family and mine had party lines and people were always interrupting and asking us to get off the phone so they could use it.

On winter days, especially when the cold was biting, the heating system at the Schule struggled to get the temperature up to 60. There were potbelly stoves in each room and they helped (although the students closest to the stoves fell asleep without fail).

An added source of heat was that Brother Edwin would come into each class and have us sing "Ich Bin Ein Musikaner," a song he taught us. And we sang it in German.

There were some teachers and there was some learning going on.

Brothers Lawrence, Leo, Marius and Edwin made us study...and want to study. Our roster, still embedded in my memory, went something like this: Andert, Barrett, Berreth, Budnik, Chlebek, Daughtery, Ernst, Farrell, Fulnecky, Gantert, Guentert, Haase, Heyge, Hertel, Hoar, Karmolinski, Kosek, Langford, Lewinski, McCarthy, Nagy, Pettit, Ruppe, Simon, Souders, Spiteri, Vargo, and Zernick.

When summer came, I spent it cutting grass, listening to the Cubs and playing tennis at Leeper Park. I worked hard enough to catch the eye of Otto "Pie" Seifert, the head tennis instructor and Director of all things tennis at Leeper Park. He was always pleasant, patient and supportive. He helped me improve my serve and backhand as well as my court sense. His coaching helped me make it through to the finals in the boys division of the South Bend Championships. I lost to Bob Pauszek, a year older than I. But I knew I'd be back.

My days at Leeper Park were peaceful and wonderful. I made friends quickly with other young tennis players, Dave and Chuck Christman, Steve Kalabany,

Dave Krizman, John Roper, Bob Wortham...the list is longer than my memory. But those clay courts, watered, rolled and lined daily by a one-armed man named Pete, were simply beautiful. And they were gentle to my bad leg, allowing me sometimes to slide into a shot I would have missed on a hard surface.

Mr. Seifert also brought important tournaments like the Western Open to the Leeper courts. Tony Trabert played there. So did Arthur Ashe and other greats. I have never for a moment forgotten Mr. Seifert's dedication to the sport of tennis and his genuine appreciation of everyone who played it. To this day I count him as a true mentor in my life.

Too soon the summer was turning to fall. My Cubs were dead last and, worse than that, had traded two of my favorite players, Andy Pafko and Johnny Schmitz to the Brooklyn Dodgers for Eddie Miksis, Gene Hermanski, the earthly remains of Lefty Joe Hatten and a couple of others. Still, my loyalty never wavered. Finishing last in the National League made it easier to to go back to school, back to Schule.

There is a special bond formed when your group has to confront mice and rookie teachers on a daily basis. We learned to bring lunch in metal pails; paper bags were easy pickings for the mice. As sophomores, we now extended that bond to the incoming freshmen. We were still in the Schule, just a bit more crowded. Some classes met in what had been the parish hall. Now we were nearly 60 strong.

But the Holy Cross Brothers countered by bringing

in a new principal from the Gary-Whiting area, Brother Reginald Justak. He was big, tough, humorless, and savvy. We had more numbers, but they had Reginald. Our freedom would have to be fought for with new methods.

We had been especially adept at driving out our religion teachers, having gone through five by the time sophomore year was over. Brother Reginald decided to bring in the heavy guns. He announced that the priest conducting our annual spiritual retreat this year would be the chaplain of the Indiana State prison in Westville. We did not flinch.

The good Fr. Westendorf began by telling us we were not too young to die. Why, two kids at a school he spoke at last year died soon thereafter. A voice from behind me whispered, "Of boredom." The prison chaplain went on to warn us about sexual sins. He said sternly, you have an obligation to quickly remove yourself from any serious occasion of sin. If you are sexually aroused, you must get away. At this point, one of our classmates raised his hand and Father called on him. "Let me get this straight, Father. If I'm in the back seat of a car with my girlfriend headed to the prom and she looks so gorgeous that I get sexually aroused, do I have to get out of the car and run alongside?" Sixty students went on a laugh binge. Brother Reginald came to the front of the room and warned us that any further disruption would be dealt with severely. He was too late; we had already won. The chaplain was probably glad to go back to the prison.

It so happened that my sophomore year marked the first time I ever kissed a girl. Her name was Suzy. We met at a mixer and liked each other enough that we shared the last dance together and I walked her home. As we neared her house, we stopped and hugged. Our faces moved toward a meeting of the lips. I actually saw my first kiss. I didn't know that your eyes were supposed to close until I saw her eyes closed. We tried a few more before I took her to her porch.

As I ran to catch the bus to go home, I remember being elated. And I might even have thought I was in love. We dated for better than a year and kissed a thousand times or more. But that was all. I did not want her to become a "near occasion of sin." As I look back, I do so with a quote in mind:

> "Outside ideas of right doing and wrong doing, there is a field.
> I'll meet you there." —*Rumi*

Sophomore year was highlighted by the installation of a Coke machine in the lunch room. One of our guys with skinny arms became very adept at reaching up the funnel, tipping loose a coke and sharing his loot with those who were cheering him on. I'm sure it bedeviled the brother who tried to figure out why the machine wasn't at least breaking even.

Perhaps we had an attitude problem. I remember being at Dave Ruppe's house when his mother, who was hosting friends for tea and bridge, saw us leaving and asked: "David, what shall I say if someone calls?" Dave replied, "Say 'hello.'"

As the school year zoomed by, we knew that this was going to be our final weeks at the Schule and we learned that Brother Reginald was already appointed principal of the new St. Joseph's High School. A new and spacious facility awaited us. And so did Brother Reginald.

The summer after sophomore year was probably the best summer of my life. I practically lived at Leeper Park, playing tennis an average of five hours a day. With coaching from "Pie" Seifert and older players, I got better every week. I practiced kill shots until they became automatic. I learned to pace myself and to detect my opponent's weaknesses so as to exploit them. By the time August arrived, so did I. Imperfect leg and arm couldn't stop me. I breezed through the first three rounds of the South Bend City Championship and set myself for the championship match. My opponent was an imposing, big, power hitter named Mike Palmer. He was clearly favored to win. But he didn't. The *South Bend Tribune* recapped the match this way:

"Palmer forced a smashing game at Langford, but the dogged champion played steady back-court tennis to win. It was a case of spirit and doggedness winning for Langford against a much harder hitter."

I don't think I can adequately describe how I felt receiving the trophy as South Bend Boys Champion. Teasing and taunting would never hurt me again. I had achieved a physical mark of excellence. Of course it was limited; South Bend was never noted as the home of great tennis players. But it was enough. Truth be told, I saw each of my opponents as representing my former bullies. As much as possible I stayed at the baseline and ran them from corner to corner just for the fun of it.

Not long after the South Bend tourney, I received a call from Bob DePree who had just won the singles title in Mishawaka. He asked me if I was going to play in the state tournament. When I said yes, he said we should join forces as a doubles team in the competition. I agreed. Bob was a really good tennis player.

In the singles competition, I won in the first round before losing to the eventual champion Bill Johnson of Evansville. But DePree and I had no trouble winning our first three matches in doubles and making it to the championship round. On the other side of the net was Bill Johnson, who had defeated both me and Bob on his way to the singles championship. His partner, George Jenkins, was from Indianapolis. I was keyed up. I desperately wanted to win the state championship. Bob and I played really well that day. There was a humorous point as well. When I challenged the call of the referee on a shot that he called "in" when it was clearly "out" he looked at me and calmly said, "Hey, Ace, keep your eyes open and your mouth shut."

We won easily, 6-2, 6-4. I will never forget how that felt. It changed me. I had held my own and my mind and heart gained a confidence and self-image I had never had before. It was a lesson I came back to, time and time again, in the unfolding of my life. It was a moment of interior actualization, a few seconds in time that borrow from eternity, a self-realization that no one could ever take this from me. It was like a temporal, brief confirmation that eternity must exist. This moment calls out the wish and the hope that it could last forever.

Later that summer I was invited to compete in the River Forest, Illinois Open tournament in the junior division. In the first round I drew Barry McKay, the top player at the University of Michigan and later a member and captain of the United States Davis Cup team. Needless to say, I was no competition for him. But he took the time to coach me through the match and it made me a better player.

In late summer there were some new faces at Leeper Park. A family named Dietsch moved to South Bend from Ohio. The three boys were tennis players and they had grown up on their own court situated on their property. They knew how to play.

No sooner had the new St. Joseph High School opened, than I was knocking on Brother Edwin Mattingly's door. As Athletic Director he was the one I had to convince to start a tennis team. We'd need a coach. I turned to Head Football Coach George Kelly, one of the finest men I ever knew. He agreed to be the nominal coach as long as I would actually be in charge of the team. We shook hands. Neither would ever be sorry.

In our first two seasons, after losing our opening match to Culver Military Academy, we went on to win 16 in a row, including, in our second year, a win over

Culver Military Academy, their first loss in four years. We were the best high school tennis team in Indiana.

The new high school at the corner of Angela Boulevard and Michigan Street was a great facility. There had been some concern if the students from Central Catholic and South Bend Catholic, strong rivals for years, would get along. It soon dawned on everyone that if you put the athletes from those schools together you would have instant powerhouses in football, basketball and baseball. What was different about the new school was that it was co-curricular. Boys, taught by brothers, had one wing; girls, taught by nuns, had a separate wing; and the administrative offices divided them. And kept them divided.

Brother Reginald tried to establish rigid discipline; we tried guerrilla tactics in response. One of the funniest incidents I remember happened when Congressman John Brademas was invited to address the student body in the gym. Brother Reginald introduced the Congressman and stepped to the side of the stage where he could observe the students in the bleachers. He spotted a student talking and laughing rather than listening. The longer it went on, the more agitated he became. Finally, unable to restrain himself, Reginald rushed across the stage, grabbed the microphone away from the Congressman and yelled, "Dygulski, just shut up!!!" Then he handed the mike back to our distinguished speaker who seemed absolutely dumbfounded.

The big change in the new school was that the faculty was more seasoned. They were better and more demanding teachers than we had experienced. St. Joe was on its way to becoming the truly great high school it is today.

My extracurricular activities in addition to tennis included being sports editor of the school paper, associate editor of the yearbook and the St. Joe reporter for the *South Bend Tribune*. In addition, I was named Catholic co-chair of the National Conference of Christians and Jews; Lucy Simon of Central High was Jewish co-chair and Marilyn Michaels of Lakeville High represented Protestants. We worked to host events supporting interfaith and inter-racial cooperation.

Meanwhile, my dating life improved immensely. Friends and I had discovered the girls at St. Mary's Academy, a boarding school for young women from all over the Midwest. It was located on what had been the vast estate of Albert Erskine, President of the Studebaker Corporation from 1915-1933.

Mixers there were monitored by nuns and chaperons; the girls there were anxious to see males. At one dance, I saw a girl who captured me at first sight. Her name was Katie. Before long I knew that I was in love for the first time. I thought she was absolutely beautiful. Happily, she lived at home in South Bend rather than on campus. That allowed us to meet almost every day at the Philadelphia Restaurant in downtown South Bend for a coke or coffee before I walked her home. We went steady for most of the next two years. I was sure I'd marry her.

The feelings of young love are powerful and they

can be ignited by a song that begs to be played over and over, or a phone call that ends with both parties saying "I love you." She built my self-esteem to new heights. I hope I did something similar for her.

The summer after my junior year brought me bad news. I got up one morning to drive my grandmother to Mass and found that my left leg was barely able to push in the clutch on our car. I attributed it to the probability that I had practiced too much tennis the day before. I wrapped a flex bandage around it and got us to church and back. But that was all. Mom could see that I didn't look well. She took my temperature and it was 104°. Dad called Dr. Nicholas Johns who came over right away. He did his various readings and examined my leg and arm on the left side, the same side that had borne the effects of my stroke at birth. I overheard him tell my parents that I had the early signs of polio. He said the temperature will remain high, he is not to move and, if necessary, we'll get him a room at the Northern Indiana Children's Hospital, a facility for polio victims.

I simply could not believe it. After all I had done to overcome my birth problem, here I was stricken again. I prayed hard. My mother took wonderful care of me. The high temperature required changing my bedding and pajamas three or four times a day. Every day for a month I lay there wondering what would happen to my life. And then, as quickly as it had taken hold of me, it let go. Dr. Johns said we can all be grateful this turned out to be abortive polio. By mid-summer I was up again, moving around, trying to regain some strength and dreaming of returning to tennis. Everyone said take it slow; be careful.

Just sitting on a bench at Leeper Park watching tennis lifted my spirits. Before long I brought my racquet and hit for 10 or 15 minutes. I was sad that I could not play in the City Championship Tournament. And then I got an idea. I called Dave Krizman, the "Human Backboard" and asked if he had a doubles partner for the tourney. He said no. I said you do now. In the first two matches, I played as much as I could and then left Dave to play the opposing team of two. He (we) won both. The next round was delayed several days by bad weather. Each day let me get stronger. Krizman carried us in the semi-finals and by the day of the championship matches, I was ready. We won.

I spent some time working out with Father Bernard Lange, the gym master at Notre Dame. He taught me the best way to lift weights.

He was a great character. Newspaper clippings on his bulletin board attested to the fact that he had once been the fourth strongest man in the world. A lot of football players worked out at his gym. If one of them or anybody else dropped a weight, he ushered them out the door. One student who suffered such an exit returned with his parents and two officers from the sheriff's department. The officers went up to notify a Vice President of the University, Father Jerry Wilson, that they were going to arrest Father Lange. Father Wilson asked, "How many men do you have in the cars?" They said, "It's just us two." Father Wilson sighed and said, "You'll need at least two more." The matter was dropped and both the sheriffs and the parents beat a quick retreat.

With polio behind me, senior year meant the happiness of Katie in my life, more serious studiousness, inventing new ways to aggravate Brother Reginald, and the completion of a 16-match winning streak in tennis. We were unquestionably the best team in the State.

Late in the spring semester I decided to enter a contest for journalism students in the Diocese of Ft. Wayne. First prize was to be a four-year scholarship to the college of your choice. First there was a two-hour test followed by the writing of a six-page article or essay. I thought I did fairly well and then forgot about it. A week later, I took the SAT tests to attach to my application for admission to the University of Notre Dame.

A month or so before graduation, Brother Reginald approached the class officers to submit ideas for the gift we would leave the school, paid for out of our class treasury, built mainly by revenues from mixers. We caucused and got back to him with our proposed legacy gift—a large, bronze wall hanging with all our names on it.

He said no thanks, that was the last thing the school needed. He had decided we'd donate a Spinet piano and that was that. A week or so later, we asked if we could hold a dance/party in the school gym right before final exams. He said no. We sent him a response signed by everyone in the graduating class that said simply "NO PARTY, NO SPINET." This time he gave in.

Our departing prank on Brother Reginald happened in the gym as we practiced the procession for graduation. In the back of the gym there was a drinking fountain. As the boys passed it, each one of us paused, took a drink, and rejoined the procession. Reginald realized we might try this on Graduation Day too, so he grabbed the mike on stage and with a grieving voice said, "Girls, pray for the boys!" It was a sentiment we immediately picked up and chanted.

Brother Reginald confessed later in life that we were his favorite class; he had secretly enjoyed our spirit and clever pranks.

Soon after graduation, it was Brother Reginald who rang the doorbell at the Langford house. My dad answered the door; I wondered what was going on. Dad called me. Reginald stuck out his hand and said, "Congratulations. You won the Journalism scholarship to college." It was a good moment and I attributed it to luck. I had been "on" that day and I had found the test easy and had left that room thinking that my essay was not bad at all.

Shortly thereafter, dad announced that we were taking a family vacation to Mexico. I tried everything to beg my way out of the trip. I pointed out that the house and grass would need to be cared for...my tennis career was blossoming. But my dad had heard my repetitive playing of romantic music and he was not about to let me stay home alone. That wisdom was confirmed every time he would bring me several letters a day from our Mexican mailbox, all perfumed, all from the same sender.

Dad promised we'd be home by mid-July and I could resume my employment at Notre Dame. Since my sophomore year in high school I spent vacations taking campus mail around the Main Building. For a while I cleaned the stoves in the kitchen of the Morris Inn. Now that I had my high school diploma, I moved up to become a campus guide for the thousands of tourists who come to see Notre Dame in the summer. I loved both jobs, especially telling tourists the story of Notre Dame. The place was already in my blood.

—3—

Notre Dame Our Mother

I had lived in the shadow of the Dome all my life. As a youngster I had often gone to campus to watch dad's tennis team practice or to go over to Cartier Field to see the football scrimmage. Coach Frank Leahy often was in the crow's nest where he could see the whole field. He had a megaphone which he used to critique each play and often order that the play be repeated until it was perfect. These were glory years for Irish football, with National Championships in '46, '47, and '49. The field was full of All-Americans and outstanding coaches.

My earliest jobs were at Notre Dame. Now here I was registering for courses!

During our time in Mexico City a few months before, I had played tennis with two players who had been recruited by Coach Charlie Samson for the Notre Dame tennis team. I played well against them and I suspect they conveyed that to Coach. No sooner had school started than he called me and said he knew I already had a journalism scholarship but he would like it if I joined his team as a walk-on. I was thrilled. Since tennis would not begin until spring, I asked my dad whether I could work out over the winter with the fencing team to get in shape for tennis. He agreed.

Academics were a struggle. I had not learned how to study in high school and college proved to be a genuine challenge. I had some wonderful teachers including Walter Gray in history, Bill Grupp in Spanish and Fr. Fred Barr in theology. The class I most disliked was swimming. Notre Dame had a rule that every student who hoped to graduate had to pass a swimming test. Classes were held in the pool of the Rockne Memorial Building. My coordination problems made swimming difficult. All I could do was the doggie paddle and side stroke. I mastered those well enough to swim the length of the pool. But then came the bigger challenges. There were probably 60 or more in my section of the class and Coach Gil Burdick wanted to make sure we could go off the high dive and to learn life-saving techniques.

The high diving board seemed a mile above us. Coach Burdick called on a basketball player to climb up to the board and make the dive. He got up to the board but decided he couldn't go through with the dive. Coach surveyed the rest of us and I could see his eyes settle on me. I tried looking the other way, but to no avail. "Langford," Coach ordered, "get up there and show what you're made of." To begin with, I'm not a friend of heights or ladders. Pride and my last name provided adrenalin enough to go, one rung after another, to the top. The steps I had to take to reach the edge of the diving board seemed like a walk to my execution. Having made it to the end of the board, I said a short prayer (as in "God help me"), took a deep breath, closed my eyes and jumped feet first. I reached the surface to hear the sound of applause from my classmates. I felt like clapping too!

The last big test was to swim to the middle of the pool and rescue a classmate who pretended to be struggling and to bring him to safety.

The guy who I was assigned to save was a fullback on the football team. I made it out to him but could not subdue his pretend panic. All I could do was to say to him: "Save yourself," as I side-stroked back to the side. Coach Burdick must have been impressed enough with my high dive that he passed me for the course.

I made lots of friends, but studying with them was a problem since I lived at home to avoid room-and-board charges on campus. I also made the staff as a sports writer for the *Notre Dame Scholastic*, the weekly student publication of news, events and features. Many of my new friends were athletes: people like Bob Williams, Al Ecuyer, Bud Reynolds, Dick Phelan, Dick

Ciesielski, Tommy Hawkins, and Gene Duffy. Others like John Paul Cannon, Joe Boland, and Terry Plunkett helped make the student experience a great one.

But I also began to wrestle in a serious way with the question: What do I want to do with my life? Did I want to be a sports writer? A lawyer? A teacher? Did I want to marry and raise a family? There were no easy answers. I thought about it carefully, talked with a counselor, visited the grotto frequently and prayed for guidance.

More and more, an answer I never expected came to me. If I was ever going to use all of my talents—speaking, writing ability, good interpersonal skills—I should consider the priesthood, at that time still an honored calling. I wanted to devote my life to something good, a cause, a vocation. I was drawn toward the priesthood.

Before I could decide with finality, I still had things to do. Late in the first semester, as the fencing season winded down, there was a tournament for freshmen, about two dozen in number, to see who would be awarded letter sweaters. Since my dad was coach, I decided to participate in epee, the only weapon that was judged electronically. Nobody could complain that I had an unfair advantage by being the coach's son.

Although epee was usually the province of tall people, I decided to cast my lot with the quickness of my right hand, a byproduct of years of use compensating for the left one. Epee was the equivalent of the old-fashioned dueling sword where the first one to draw blood was declared the winner. My stance was more like a knife fighter than a classic fencing pose. And I worked my way through three rounds and won the monogram. Dad was observing from afar...but I caught him checking out my efforts. I think I surprised him.

It was very funny when my football friends and I would wear our letter sweaters going to a game or a dance. People would sort of stare at me walking with all these big men and I overheard one guy say, "He must be fast." Having won my sweater in fencing, I decided not to go out for tennis.

Late in the fall, I was working out at Father Lange's gym and decided that I would, that very day, accept the challenge he had posted on the wall: "One man in every 200,000 can press his weight." I only weighed 130 pounds at the time and I knew I could press more than 100 pounds. I told Father I was ready. He seemed pleased and set up the weights. With a struggle I managed the 100 and 110. But as I lifted the 120 pounds, I felt something give in my abdomen. I set the weight down. I knew what it was. Later that day, Dr. Green confirmed that I had a hernia. It was only a few days before Christmas vacation. I spent four days of that special time in the hospital for hernia surgery.

No more weights for me. I resolved to be among the 199,999 who were losers.

As the second semester wound down, I learned that I had been promoted to Assistant Sports Editor of the *Scholastic*, with a line of advancement to Sports Editor and then possibly Editor-in-Chief...there was journalism again demanding my attention.

In April, even before school was out, my gaze toward the priesthood grew more focused. I sent a letter to the Director of Vocations for the central province of the Dominican Order, more formally known as the Order of Preachers, asking for an application to join.

The Order was founded in 1216 by St. Dominic Guzman, a Spaniard whose life embodied zeal, risk taking, faith and courage.

The Dominican motto is: "To contemplate and give to others the fruits of that contemplation." Dominic wanted his followers to be scholars, teachers, preachers and missionaries. I read books about the Order and its saints and I decided I wanted to be one of them. My mother's brother was a Dominican; he wanted me to join. So did my mom, with reservations. "You will always be welcomed home if it doesn't work out." But my dad was not as confident that this was the life I should embrace. Perhaps he knew me better than any of the others did, and his realistic view of me was more level-headed than the one that prevailed. I think he knew I was not mature enough, deep enough, to make this decision for all my life.

My friends were dumbfounded. Katie bet me five dollars I wouldn't last. Aside from me there were no takers. The decision meant giving up my scholarship to Notre Dame and leaving those I loved to walk a path that promised more thorns than palm leaves along the way. But I had tasted a lot of what life could offer and the idealistic side of me saw it as a chance to find happiness by complete devotion to serving others.

The Dominicans had a very wise rule that you could not enter the novitiate and become a full member without completing two years of college. The vocation director told me to do my sophomore year at Loras College in Dubuque, Iowa, and to take several courses in Latin, creative writing, German and literature. They agreed that I could play on the Loras tennis team. I loved Dubuque, located on the Mississippi River and my year at Loras was a good one. I went home for the summer, my last before the monastic and studious life that awaited me. Again I worked as a guide on the Notre Dame campus. When the time came, I said my goodbyes to friends and experienced excitement as I looked to what lay ahead.

When the end of August arrived, my parents drove me to Union Station in South Bend for the ride first to Chicago and then on the Burlington Northern to Winona, Minnesota. My goodbye was filled with emotions: love, gratitude, hope and excitement. More than half of the 400-mile train route provided views of the Mississippi River. It was beautiful.

When the train stopped at Winona, I stepped down the stairs with a prayer for my new life. A cleric in a black suit and Roman collar met me and asked if I was Jim. I said yes. He responded, "From now on, your name is Jerome. Welcome, Brother Jerome." The idea behind changing your name was that you were now in a new life; the old life was left behind, name and all.

What lay ahead began with 365 straight days in the novitiate of St. Peter Martyr, a gothic, stone building located on 60 or so acres, high on a hill west of Winona. It was away from everything. In the distance you could see the Mississippi River.

It was a full year away from the world. Only occasional visitors were allowed and only immediate family. There were no newspapers, no television, no radios. We spent hours each day in the chapel, learning Gregorian chant, chanting the divine office, Mass, praying the rosary and meditating. We wore the tunics and scapular of monks. The day began at 5:30 a.m. and ended by 9 p.m.

For the most part, silence was the rule, broken only by an hour for recreation and perhaps two hours doing farm chores. Weather permitting, outside recreation was baseball or football.

Each novice had a private room, very simply furnished with a bed, small closet, table, lamp and sink. Rooms were completely private; only the occupant and, if needed, the infirmarian could enter. Silence was the rule, solemn silence after lights out. Once a week there was a chapter of faults where, one by one, the novices acknowledged misdeeds and faults in front of the whole community. Late arrival at chapel required the novice to lie on the stone floor until the Prior knocked, allowing him to rise and take his place in the choir stalls.

Everyone received a daily assignment of duties cleaning and maintaining the Priory. Letters going out and coming in were opened and read by the Novice Master. Much of the year found us on a diet of fasting and abstinence from meat. Once I got used to the routine I grew to like it, even the incredible amount of praying, perhaps five hours a day. The point of all this was to foster discipline, spiritual growth and a new understanding of humility.

Every member of our class had finished two years or more of college. One was an army veteran, one a lawyer, and several were accomplished athletes. That two-year requirement was a blessing; we had each experienced some of life's offerings and that led to more maturity among the novices than many seminaries could offer.

It goes without saying that in any group of recruits there will be a variety of personalities and foibles. In addition, the novice master, Father John Connell, seemed to be uncomfortable in his own skin. He compensated by being so pious that he made everybody feel uncomfortable. It was not too long before sensing that we all needed more comic relief, I called on my skill for imitating voices and gestures. I could imitate the Prior to a tee and the novice master well enough to turn our half-hour of recreation into a comedy show. I later found out that he had a two-way speaker that allowed him to hear every one of my performances.

I believed then, as I do now, that religion and spirituality are fed, not obstructed, by humor. They do not require being somber. Holiness should lead to smiles, not to sanctimonious observances. Law and rules are necessary, but the letter of the law can squelch the spirit.

My most egregious misstep happened in the

summer when Brother Gerald I and donned parkas and entered the walk-in freezer to feast on frozen chocolate mint cookies. We would have gone undetected except for the red light outside the freezer door that indicated someone was in there. Of course it was Fr. Connell who caught us. I confessed it at the next Chapter of Faults, once again drawing laughter.

On occasion I was the butt of jokes as well. When any member of our Province died, his body was brought to the graveyard at our Priory. I was assigned to the gravedigger squad. We had two funerals, several months apart. Unfortunately, we dug too close to the previous burial and I was five feet down there when the wall caved in. I used the shovel almost as a pole vault in my frantic effort to reach the surface. It took months to live down the imitations of my scurry to the top.

But my year in the novitiate wasn't play. It was the beginning of a long wrestling match between nature and grace in me. I truly wanted to be holy and happy at the same time.

You don't grow spiritually because you want to or because you think your efforts can earn it. It takes grace, and grace is a gift of God, not a reward for human effort. Grace doesn't overcome human nature; it completes it.

I experienced a deepening sense of God, in part by reading and re-reading the Scriptures, in part by meditating and praying more with appreciation and gratitude than with requests. I felt I belonged here and that I should finish the year by taking vows of poverty, chastity and obedience for a three-year period. Once those vows were made it would be time to move to the next step. The 14 of us who survived the novitiate were now to move to the Dominican House of Studies in River Forest, Illinois. We would be joining a much larger community made up of the second-and third-year students, the faculty and the brothers who took care of the building and premises, which work was part of their vocation and commitment.

The building was impressive, centered around the chapel, with a large refectory, several stories worth of classrooms, private rooms for the students, a library, and a grand recreation facility dominated by a large fireplace. The whole place had a monastic tone about it...simple, expertly designed, conducive to a context in which we could further our understanding and inculcate a love of knowledge that could inform and inspire our life and our future ministry. The rooms for students were spartan but more than adequate. A bed, sink, closet, desk and lamp were enough.

The first week of classes was both exhilarating and intimidating. Every class but one or two was taught in Latin, the texts were in Latin and exams too. All that study of Latin at Loras proved to be not a luxury, but a necessity. The faculty was brilliant and most were good teachers. It quickly became apparent that they were teaching us how to study and inspiring us to want to study. Every day was filled by classes, chapel and a little recreation.

No one would have predicted I would fall in love with philosophy, but I did. I studied as I had never studied before. We were learning a system of thinking about life, nature, ethics, and the abstract, but real, truths and principles that make it all work. Our primary guides were Aristotle and Thomas Aquinas and we poured over their works as primary sources, aided by the contexts of the history of philosophy, the insights of other systems, and the precepts of sound logic. There were courses on ethics, metaphysics, history of philosophy, methodology, cosmology, logic, psychology, and philosophy of religion. The reason Latin was used was so that we could study basic texts in the language in which they were written. And, in some ways, it was more exact in meaning than other languages are.

I discovered an ability to focus I never knew I had. It was not about memorizing definitions to do well on tests. It was about understanding and owning the concepts and their interactive role in absorbing parts of a mosaic that was a complete, all-embracing philosophy. There were light-bulb moments when a concept became clear enough to prompt a "Eureka!"

In my mind, the more you know, the more you are able to love, the more you are able to teach, lead, stand for, and not stand for. From day one my studies were totally geared to my future ministry.

By far, the greatest scholar on the faculty was Fr. James A. Weisheipl. In addition to a doctorate from the Angelicum in Rome, he earned a doctorate in the history of science at Oxford. His specialties were the history of philosophy, history of science, and all things Medieval. He was totally devoted to being a Dominican scholar. He earned an international reputation for his publications and his scholarship. Still in my first year of philosophy, he identified me as a student with the potential to become a scholar and a writer.

I latched on to his brilliance, diligence and inspiration. He often would be found in the Priory book bindery, where he carefully restored centuries-old treatises. Notebook and pen in hand, I followed his words as he carefully described the origins of modern science and demonstrated the role of medieval thought in that development. He led me to the best sources of more knowledge on particular aspects. It opened a world of thought and history I had never known existed.

All along, Father Weisheipl had a major project in mind for me. He wanted to train me so that I could research and write a balanced and accurate account of Galileo and his confrontations with authorities in the Church. I used one aspect or another of the Galileo affair for nearly every paper I would write in any and every course over the next six years.

Something in me adapted fully to this monastic kind of life. I can't say that I didn't miss girls, dating and the excitement of sharing affection. I did. But I immersed myself in study and prayer and resigned my mind to the fact that there had to be sacrifices to reach what I believed to be my calling. We formed good friendships within the community and that seemed to be enough.

I am guessing my happiness quotient was nine out of a possible ten. My only major disappointment was that I didn't know what to expect in terms of a relationship with God. I wasn't looking for a miraculous conversion or the inner ecstasy of a saint. All I wanted was some sense that I was doing what God wanted me to do.

I was often moved by the beauty of chanting with 75 male voices whose echoes seemed to sing back from the Gothic ceiling. Prayer, meditation and study were my links and lifelines to God.

My second year studying philosophy was much like the first. My parents, and sometimes old friends, would come to visit when visits were allowed. Otherwise, we stayed in touch by mail. One of my good friends from high school, Bob Spiteri, smuggled in a very small battery-operated radio. I broke the rules by hiding it in a pocket under my robes. Bob was a fellow Cubs fan and he knew how much I wanted to have some connection during the baseball season. One day in the summer I played it too loudly and it was confiscated.

Studies and tutoring by my mentor went very well. I think my parents were surprised by how well I was doing. A sub-par high school education and very average college career suddenly blossomed: I graduated with a B.A. in Philosophy *summa cum laude*—with highest honors. Now it was time to spend one more year to earn a master's degree in philosophy and to complete the period of three-year vows in favor of lifetime vows.

My master's thesis was titled "the Condemnation of Galileo," and it was well received and published by the Lyceum for Philosophy and Science. The required exam was conducted in Latin by a three-person faculty board. I did well enough to earn my degree *magna cum laude*. An additional honor came with the conferral of a Ph.Lic....from the Pontifical Faculty, a degree licensing me to teach philosophy at any Catholic university or college in the world.

So far as I could tell, this was the life for which I was chosen, and had myself chosen, to live.

I was sad to be leaving River Forest, but glad to take final vows and move on to the Aquinas Institute of Theology in Dubuque, Iowa, for four years of intensive study of theology and gradual reception of Holy Orders leading to the priesthood. My family was there for the vows ceremony and my Mom made sure to tell me that if I decided to come home instead, they would welcome me with open arms. Several of my friends did not take the vows and went home. That was the only sad part of the day for me.

St. Rose Priory in Dubuque was a large, recently built red brick structure, sitting in the countryside above the city below. You could not see the Mississippi, but you knew it was there. The rules and regimen were pretty much what we were used to, but we were allowed a bit more freedom, including junkets to the river in a group of four or five to rent a rowboat, find an island in the river, and relax with beer and a sandwich. I joined the groups as often as I could; I loved the river and the warmth of the sun.

The studies were as challenging as those at River

Forest, but with the added dimension that they related directly to the study of God, Scripture, Ethics, Ecclesiology, Grace, Pastoral Counseling, Public Speaking, and Canon Law. We also took beginning courses in Hebrew and Greek as those related to Scripture. I don't care what the class was, in the back of my mind there always lurked the story of Galileo and Father Weisheipl's expectation that I would write a definitive study of his difficulties with the Church.

Although the Aquinas Institute's library had a remarkable collection of seventeenth-century works, several of which yielded contemporary comments on Galileo and detailed rules about detainment and procedures of the Holy Office in the seventeenth century, I wanted more. My pleas were heard and I was sent to the Dominican House of Studies in Washington, D.C. for the summer so that I could work with books and documents at the Library of Congress. What a great thrill it was to spend hours every day engrossed in works I needed. There was no Xerox machine at the time so everything I found useful needed to be copied carefully and accurately by hand. Since Galileo wrote in Italian more than in Latin, I had to learn enough Italian to let me understand the important passages I wanted to use. I take some pride in the fact that to this day some of my translations have entered the literature and been cited in subsequent books.

In theology, we used the critical-thinking skills we had learned in philosophy and applied them to better understand the Scriptures, divine attributes and human action. The goal was to broaden knowledge, to provide insights for meditation and contemplation and to arm us for the work we would be doing as teachers and preachers. But life within the confines of the Priory still had room for pranks and humor.

The Priory property included five acres of mature woods that were perfect for quiet walks, especially when they blazed their fall coat of many colors. One afternoon on a walk, I spotted a multi-colored bird, the size of a chicken, on the path ahead. Its red breast was topped by a tiger-spotted neck leading to a shiny gold crown. I had never seen anything like it. When I returned to the Priory I did some research and discovered that it was a Chinese Golden pheasant. I looked for it every time I walked there and it seemed we got used to each other. As days and weeks went by the pheasant let me get closer before darting away from me. I enlisted the help of a couple of classmates and, with the aid of a tennis net, we were able to capture it. No hunter would get this bird! We named him Lagrange, in honor of the great Dominican scripture scholar M.J. Lagrange. The Prior thought it seemed harmless enough so we were allowed to keep Lagrange, to build him a shelter, fence it in, and occasionally to bring him into a handball court in the basement of the building. Over the winter we actually tamed Lagrange. But in the spring, Lagrange could not help himself and he earned his exile. Every morning he would wake up an entire wing of the Priory with his loud, insistent mating call. He could even be heard in the chapel.

Mating calls have no place in the halls of a monastery. We were told to release him, which we did, with sadness.

In our third year of study at the Priory I decided to pull a prank that would have brought a smile to my old high school principal Brother Reginald's face.

Our Professor of Canon Law was a unique character who also worked in the Marriage Tribunal of the Archdiocese of Dubuque. Part of his assignment, as he perceived it, was to make sure that everyone getting close to ordination knew about the varieties of sexual sins so we would know how to deal with them in the confessional. He made it difficult for the students by studying faces to see how each reacted to his blunt recital of possibilities. If you smiled, he would exclaim that you were guilty of "morose delectation." If you tried to be expressionless, he saw you as uncaring and too stern. He was a native of Kentucky and spoke with a kind of redneck accent. His nickname was "Jughead." I decided to prank him.

Every night, just as darkness descended, Jughead would take a walking stick and, dressed in ragtag clothes, walk around the outside of the entire Priory several times. I told all the students to be on the alert and looking out the windows on this particular evening about eight o'clock. At quarter of, I called the police, identified myself as the Prior, and reported that there was some strange vagabond person stalking the Priory. We watched with absolute delight as the police pulled up, lights flashing, and stopped Jughead. You could see him arguing with them and then they walked him to the front door and asked for the Prior to come out and identify him. It's the kind of story you really had to be there to appreciate fully.

As the school year wound down, in addition to completing a Master's degree in theology, we were taught the proper way to say Mass. That brought home in a dramatic way that finally we would be ordained priests. It had been eight years since I signed up and gone to Loras College. I was now 27 years old. My life-long friends back home were married with children a home, and a car. But I had persevered and my dream, my goal, was about to be realized.

— 4 —

Tu est Sacerdos in Aeternum

*T*o live in the midst of the world
without wishing its pleasures;
To be a member of each family,
yet belonging to none;
To share all suffering;
to penetrate all secrets;
To heal all wounds;
to go from men to God
and offer Him their prayers;
To return from God to men
to bring pardon and hope;
To have a heart of fire for Charity,
and a heart of bronze for Chastity;
To teach and to pardon,
console and bless always.
My God, what a life;
and it is yours,
O priest of Jesus Christ.

This encomium, penned by the 19th-century French Dominican preacher H.B. Henri Lacordaire, said well why I hoped to be a priest and why my day of ordination was such an indescribable day for me. My heart was filled to overflowing with gratitude to the God I intended to serve and to everyone who had guided me, inspired me, admonished me and laughed with me in the seven years it took to get from the train station in Winona, Minnesota, to now lying face down on the cold marble floor in the Sanctuary of St. Rose Priory in Dubuque, Iowa, waiting for the Bishop to complete the rite of ordination. I felt at peace, but otherwise not any different, not like St. Paul being knocked off his horse. It was hard to believe that this day, this moment, was finally here. I did not feel large and proud, I had a sense of being small and humble. I did not get here by myself. It was indeed a day of celebration, mainly a shared thanksgiving for the grace that had singled us out to accept a life of service in love.

As was customary, each new priest could now raise his hands over the head of his parents—or those who had raised him—and extend, on behalf of God, these words while making the sign of the Cross:

"May the blessing of Almighty God, Father, Son and Holy Spirit, descend upon you and remain forever."

The rest of the day was spent with family and friends sharing plans for the trip back to South Bend where I would say my first Mass in the church where I had first been raised: Holy Cross.

The trip back to South Bend was joyous and filled with news and good wishes. It was almost overwhelming.

Entering our family home was both familiar and strange. The furniture and rooms all looked the same as they had seven years ago.

But I felt more detached, like it was some kind of time warp I couldn't enter. So much had happened since I was last there; the place itself and my loved ones hadn't changed. But I had.

The few days at home were a welcome rest, punctuated by the thrill of saying Mass and preaching from the pulpit in Sacred Heart Church at Notre Dame. I remember that experience warmly and vividly every time I go into that Church.

I cherished my time with family and friends. A number of my high school buddies jokingly asked whether I'd hear their confession and I said, no, I already know what you'd confess and if you think I'd go light on the penance, think again.

As much as I enjoyed being "home," I was not sad to go back to St. Rose Priory for my final year of theological study. We were now priests. Since I had already added a Masters degree and a Lectoratus degree in theology to my degrees in philosophy, I was now more interested in practical theology, counseling and preaching.

Back in Dubuque, all of the newly ordained priests were sent out on Sundays to say Mass and preach at parishes within 50 miles that needed the help. It was a great experience and I thoroughly enjoyed it. But I also relished the time I had to go over my Galileo manuscript and to make additions or changes one final time before trying to find a publisher. I thought about sending it to Sheed and Ward or Paulist Press, but a fellow Dominican told me his dad worked as an editor at the Mentor division of New American Library, a very large and respected New York publishing house. The fact that it was an even-handed study, based on extensive research and told in a communicative voice, meant that it might be received poorly by ultra conservatives in the Church as well as seasoned critics of the Church who had beaten the dead horse of the Galileo case for decades, if not centuries.

I had been warned that I should prepare for a long search and many rejection letters. So I was really unprepared for the letter that came about a month after submission. It was from Bill Birmingham, chief editor of Mentor Omega Books. It said: "We think your book is important and well done and we want to publish it." With the letter was a contract.

I called Father Weisheipl to tell him the good news and to thank him for having inspired, mentored and supported the project. I was 28 years old and here I was the author of a book I could never have imagined writing. New American Library sold the hardcover rights to Desclee, a French publisher trying to make inroads in the American market. The book was very well received and positively reviewed.

Subsequent history has told an incredible story:

Galileo, Science and the Church is currently in its third edition, having been in print steadily since 1966. The Desclee edition was followed by a long and continuing run with Ann Arbor Paperbacks at the University of Michigan Press. It has become a standard in the vast literature on Galileo and has been used in courses at more than 40 colleges and universities. To this day I am amazed by its reception and longevity.

I was exhilarated and hoping that the superiors in the Province would grant my request to further my studies in Renaissance science, philosophy and theology at the University of Padua. At that point, I was willing and hoping to spend my priestly life mainly as a scholar and teacher. But the Province had recently instituted a rule that anyone headed for post-graduate studies had first to prove their communicative skills by teaching in a college. I asked for an exemption from that new rule, arguing that there was a side of me that really wanted to put the academic life on the back burner and to serve people more directly through preaching, counseling, and teaching. I was afraid that I would so love the active ministry that I would not want to go back to the pursuit of scholarship.

I could not convince them.

My first assignment was to study clinical psychology as a temporary staff member at the State Mental Hospital in Independence, Iowa (now called The Mental Health Institute), and then to join the faculty of theology at St. Thomas College (now St. Thomas University), then an all-male college in St. Paul, Minnesota.

The aftermath of that assignment changed the course of my life.

I don't know where to start in telling the story of the next several months. I remember the hospital as a gigantic building consisting of a central area, five stories high, with two adjoining wings, three stories each. There were rooms for about 180 patients, plus some staff and interns. It was built in the late 1800s and there is no doubt that, in its 75 years, it had hosted thousands and thousands of people who were broken by a litany of sad, traumatic experiences.

Those of us who were there to learn by helping had rooms on a third-floor section. We could hear the cries and screams at night coming from the rooms below us.

After a day of indoctrination, we were each assigned a roster of patients, in my case, 24. I was given a file on each patient that offered a concise account of their life, the events that led to their hospitalization, the intake evaluation, and subsequent entries from the staff doctor in charge of their case. My assignment was to become familiar with all the information on my patients and to visit each one every day, making observations and recording them. There were regular staff meetings during which each patient and his or her treatment was discussed. I liked these meetings because I was eager to know how my patients were perceived by professionals and what prognosis was made for each. I did not feel hesitant to speak up, whether to ask a question or to supply my own take on what the daily visits had told me.

I also sat in on intake meetings where each new patient appeared before a board of staff members who asked questions, especially about the events that led to their commitment. When the interview was finished and the door closed, the staff offered their diagnoses and tried to reach a consensus on how to classify the illness and what program might be set up for treatment.

I vividly remember one intake meeting that left me perplexed.

A middle-aged man was brought in by the sheriff who reported that his wife had called and claimed he was acting wild with anger and threats and that she wanted him committed. When confronted by the sheriff, he nearly went berserk. Now here he was, facing a panel who wanted to categorize his specific diagnosis. He yelled at us and said that it was his wife who was unbalanced and that she had beaten him to the phone and committed him before he could do so to her. Who wouldn't be angry at being hauled away while the real person needing help remained home? Was he suffering from undifferentiated schizophrenia with a psychotic episode, or was he justifiably out of control? A social worker was assigned to investigate his claims. Two days later, the evidence was presented; he was released and we met his wife who was now the one committed. I began to wonder how I would have reacted had I been in his shoes. That made his response seem mild.

As I came to know my patients and to learn their stories, the neat, orderly, rationally explicable universe became challenged and soon began to crumble.

Everything that I had learned and accepted in a total system now came face-to-face with the reality of unreasoning and the power of an existential view that could accept bits and pieces without major concern for how they might be combined in a grand picture.

My patients, at least most of them, also became my friends. I ached for them and they accepted my presence to them as something good. I learned that some of their fantasies...like seeing men dressed in yellow raincoats on the roof of the hospital...were real to them. It was not surprising that the young woman, who had been regularly abused sexually by her own grandfather, withdrew from reality in order to survive the horrors that had been done to her.

Perhaps the most interesting and humorous was a woman who had earned a Ph.D. at the University of Chicago in Near Eastern Studies. I was warned that she would be difficult. When I met her for the first time, she informed me that we would not have a conversation in any language except Hebrew, Aramaic or Greek. Subsequently she softened enough to speak English. One time, when she disagreed with something I had said, she retorted: "I'm in here not because of ignorance, but because of insanity." That seemed like an admirable distinction until watching a recent political ad made me realize that it's not a good distinction at all. One can be both!

At the end of every day, I retired to my room to think and pray. Could the perfect orderly and understandable system of Aristotle and St. Thomas possibly account for what tortured these good souls every day of their lives? Where was the line that separated those who didn't have to come here because they found ways to cope, and those who were here because they couldn't? Was mental illness innate, self-initiated or forced? Where was divine grace or intervention in all of this? What chance did those we cared for have to recover? Ever?

I began to see that the magnificent philosophical-theological system I had embraced no longer had all the answers. It has always remained my point of reference, but in the places and ways where it seemed to be wanting, I began to search elsewhere for understanding or more applicable insights. It didn't involve seeking a whole new worldview, just making corrections, alterations and limitations to the one I held.

At that point I needed to feed my spirit. I started reading the works of Fr. Pierre Teilhard de Chardin, the French Jesuit paleontologist whose grand vision for past and future was based on what he saw as evidence for his argument that, like it or not, everything was conspiring to lead all people and things of the world closer and closer to unity. In his view, evolution didn't stop with the advent of mankind, but rather we continue to evolve toward a Christ-centered communion he called the Omega Point. The Vatican banned his works from seminary libraries because they seemed too focused on the growth of goodness and not enough on the failures of human nature. I didn't try to borrow copies of Chardin's writings from seminary libraries; I bought my own at bookstores. They included *The*

Phenomenon of Man, The Divine Milieu, Hymn of the Universe, and *The Future of Man.*

I found his work energizing, hope-building and spiritually refreshing. Perhaps it was, in part, the fact that his books were such a strong antidote to the sadness of the hospital. Whatever it was that touched me, I took Chardin's message with me and it came to play a role in a subsequent issue with the administrators of the college whose faculty I was soon to join.

I had several favorites at the Hospital. One was a fellow who lived with the fear that the United States government was out to get him. When I asked why they were searching for him, he said that he had loaned 20 million dollars to President Roosevelt for the war effort and that the government didn't want to pay it back. In fact, he pointed out, they never even bothered to answer any of his letters. He played out his paranoia by wearing a tan trench coat and hiding behind one tree after another when he was outside during recreation. Although he never spotted any government operatives, he suspected that one day he would.

When he heard that my time as his confidant was up, he summoned me over to his tree. Quietly, he thanked me, assured me that he would remain vigilant, and then gave me a note which, he said, I should use if I were ever in trouble. Later, I opened it. It said, above his signature, simply, "This guy is OK." I carried that with me for many years until I lost my wallet. But the sentiment remains with me still.

Though sad to leave my patients, I was excited to

go back to Dubuque, pack my belongings, head to Minneapolis and get to work.

—5—

The Beginning and The End

As I boarded the Burlington Zephyr for the trip from Dubuque to the Twin Cities, I could not help but recall my last trip on these tracks... from Chicago to Winona, from my old life to my new one. Here I was, about to be a college teacher and a minister. Pretty heavy things to think about as I looked out at beautiful views of the Mississippi River which guided us north, along the same route as the Burlington but well past Winona into central Minnesota.

My luggage, safely aboard, consisted of a couple of suitcases and a medium-sized box. Technically, the vow of poverty meant that we really didn't own anything; everything was community property and we were just using it. My wardrobe was simple: a black suit, Roman collar, some tee shirts, black wash pants and sweaters, two Dominican habits and so forth. The box held my books, notes, family pictures, writing instruments and the like.

Although I was now to be a member of the St. Thomas College faculty, I was assigned to live at the Dominican Priory connected to Holy Rosary Church located at 2424 18th Avenue South, Minneapolis. It was an old parish and Priory, located in a neighborhood not far south of downtown. The area was peopled by Native Americans, Blacks, Hispanics and poor Whites. The average income level was under the poverty line. Right across the street was South High School, with a reputation for being less than a teacher's delight.

There were eight priests and a brother living in Holy Rosary Priory. I was much younger than any of them. I was shown to my room on the second floor and given a copy of the Priory schedule. Community recitation of the Divine Office, Mass, breakfast, more Divine Office before lunch, then lunch, then nothing until the cocktail half-hour and dinner and then either personal time or community time watching television.

Obviously I would be absent much of the day, teaching and counseling at St. Thomas.

There was a fellow Dominican teaching at St. Thomas, an intelligent, personable priest, Cajetan Fiore. He lived in the other Dominican Priory in Minneapolis, St. Albert the Great Priory and parish. Though just a mile or so south of Holy Rosary, that parish had a different demographic and a much more active staff.

The theology faculty at St. Thomas consisted of 10 or 11 members, all priests, most experienced. The chair of the department was Fr. Walter Peters, a kind and capable leader.

I was assigned to teach three sections of a course on Sacred Scripture. I wanted to do it well and I prepared diligently. The syllabus contained a number of books, some required, some as collateral reading. The first semester was to study the Hebrew Testament and the second semester would seek to understand the New Testament.

Although I tried to play it cool as I walked into my first class, inside I was excited and hopeful. I decided that the students might as well get used to me early, announcing that, in preparation for teaching at St. Thomas College, I had spent the summer working at a state mental hospital. The kids enjoyed the humor. We were off to a good start. I passed out the syllabus and offered some assurance that doing the readings, joining the discussions, and being prepared for tests would be the keys to success in this course.

It didn't take long for me to know how much I enjoyed teaching, and my students. St. Thomas was and is a very good school; the same can be said of the student body. Before long, I split lunchtime between the faculty dining room and the student dining hall.

My office was in O'Shaughnessy Hall which had been a gift from I.A. O'Shaughnessy, the same man who donated O'Shaughnessy Hall at Notre Dame. My dad's office was in that hall and I had taken classes there during my freshman year. I found now having my office in this O'Shaughnessy Hall a happy coincidence. In fact, my office was just down the hall from that of Bishop James Shannon, president of the college, a fact that will come into play later in the story.

I often stayed on campus for an hour or two after classes were finished. That allowed me to have office hours and be available to the students. It also allowed me to avoid an early return to Holy Rosary Priory and the stale negativity it embodied on a daily basis. If I didn't make it there before the 5:00 race through the Divine Office prayers, the Prior was sure to ask me where I'd been. I wanted to tell him that I had been fulfilling my ministry, unlike my confreres who, after napping, rose to watch reruns of "Jeopardy" on TV. Yes, they were on time for prayer and that seemed enough to justify their ministerial inactivity.

Early in the spring semester, I was invited to fill the vacant position of St. Thomas tennis coach. Since my teaching salary was paid to the Priory and this additional job would add to that salary, permission from the Prior was quickly forthcoming. My monthly spending allowance of $15.00 from the Priory was not increased. Given my coaching duties, I usually missed the pre-dinner prayers. Apparently now they could get by without me.

St. Thomas College is a member of the Minnesota Intercollegiate Athletic Conference (division 3). The tennis team I inherited had finished 1-8 in the prior year. I had to work with the returning players plus any freshmen who would join us. We practiced after classes every afternoon. As we got closer to our first match of the season, I ran a tournament to see which players would emerge. We had three above-average players and in our first season together our record improved to 4-5.

More important than the record was the bond the players formed with each other and with the coach. It was fun. Names like Mike McDonough, Dick Coleman, Chuck Magera, and Dennis Esterbrook would never be found on the roster of great tennis players, but they ranked high on my list of good competitors and good people. Since I practiced with the team, I found myself regaining some of my former skills. It was fun.

As the school year wound down, I was eager to receive my assignment for the summer. I hoped it would not leave me at Holy Rosary. It didn't! I was to spend the summer back in River Forest and teach courses at Rosary College for the next 10 weeks.

I was also told that I would return to St. Thomas College in the fall and that my new teaching partner would be Father John McCarthy.

John had been an All-American-caliber basketball star at Notre Dame, a professional tennis player, great student, and genuinely fine person To top it off, I'd now have an ally at Holy Rosary. I decided not to say much about the Priory to John. Let him make his own observations. His years as an outstanding athlete had taught him to be both tough and patient. I shared the being tough aspect more than the patient one, but had neither to the degree he did.

I enjoyed living for the summer back at the House of Studies in River Forest and teaching at Rosary, but it was exciting to be going back to St. Thomas. This year I would be teaching both Scripture and Ethics courses. I didn't realize it, but it was to be the most challenging year of my life.

In retrospect, I spent time and effort contemplating on my personal need to live up to my calling. The word "Veritas"—Truth—is emblazoned on the Dominican shield. I began to realize that Pere Lacordaire's praise of the priesthood seemed out of reach for me. I knew that I was appreciated for my preaching, and I happily accepted the invitation to preach a two-day retreat for students and faculty at St. Teresa's College in Winona. I knew I had the attention of my students, several of whom subsequently joined the Dominican Order. My work in the parish, preaching, counseling, hearing confessions was a joy. I remember hearing a confession that was like a recitation of sins from a list. When I asked the penitent, who seemed to be in his late teens, why his listing of sins seemed so mechanical, he said he had found a list in the prayer books in the pews of the church. I explained that what he should do in confession was to reflect the state of his soul, the successes and failures of his attempt to live life as a Christian. When it came time to assign him a penance, I told him that he was to rip that page out of the prayer book in the first two pews. He replied, "Really?" I said, "Yes."

What was sadly lacking was being part of a

community that could read Lacordaire's encomium without embarrassment. I had envisioned living with a group of friars who would seek every opportunity to extend, deepen and serve the faithful. Rather than encouragement and helpful advice from the older priests, John and I were subjected to constant criticism because we did not buy into the do-the-minimum standard that they had the authority to enforce.

I knew myself well enough to know that, if subjected long enough to that attitude, I might some day let my zeal slide into mediocrity and become tied to a routine that included obstructing and demeaning the efforts of others. This was not the apostolate I had envisioned nor the kind of priest I had vowed to become.

Saying all this may legitimately open me to charges of being judgmental, holier-than-thou, and insensitive to what these priests faced in their lives. There may be at least an element of truth in these charges. But that is how I felt. And the feeling was unrelenting.

In the fall, it was announced that the College of St. Thomas would conduct a study, department by department, of the curriculum and course list of each. The entire faculty would meet to hear the reports and recommendations that would then be put to a vote by the entire faculty.

Father Walter Peters, chair of theology, requested our input. I asked Fr. Peters to include a course I wanted to teach on the thought of Teilhard de Chardin. His works were being widely discussed at the time and I pointed out that they would certainly stimulate student interest in theology. The department faculty agreed with me.

Since every other department had seen its curricular changes proposed, discussed and accepted, we did not anticipate the ruckus that would result from our request.

What ensued was a spirited debate in front of the entire faculty of the College. Many of the priests who were not in our department objected to several proposed courses, most vehemently to mine on Teilhard de Chardin. Fr. Marvin O'Connell of the history department decried the absence of more courses on the thought of St. Thomas Aquinas and pointed out his amazement that a Dominican (me) would champion Chardin over Aquinas. He labeled it a sad attempt to hop on a bandwagon. When I responded, I pointed out that it might be better to be on a 20th-century bandwagon than an Aristotelian oxcart. I'm sure the lay faculty members were amazed and entertained to see the debate continue. I pointed out that no one tried to tell the Physics department what to offer to its students, or the English department or History department and so on. In theory at least, simply because they were priests did not make them theologians, which presumably the College hired us to be.

At a certain point the debate was halted by Monsignor William O'Donnell, Academic Vice President and Dean of the College. He called for a vote from the faculty. Since I felt that some high percentage of the lay faculty would side with us, I asked that the vote be confidential rather than by a show of hands, thus avoiding the possibility of reprisal. My request was denied. Even at that, a majority of lay faculty stood with us. We lost by two votes, and were directed to submit a revised curriculum within a week. Monsignor O'Donnell announced: "We are not ashamed of anything done here today."

I took him at his word. That evening I called a friend on the staff of the *National Catholic Reporter* and told him the story.

Two days later it was retold in print in the NCR with the slant that the rejection of Chardin was a wrongful attempt to enforce a narrow view of orthodoxy and a slap in the face of academic freedom.

The day after the article was published, I received a telegram from Bishop Shannon saying he wanted to see me in his office. The telegram was a little over the top since his office was just down the hall from mine. I immediately headed down the hall.

As I was ushered into his presence, he looked up and said: "Finding out who leaked the story to the NCR is like tracking elephants in snow." I said, "Of course it was me. Monsignor O'Donnell said we need not be ashamed of anything we did here. I took him at his word."

He said that I had earned a strong following among the students for my teaching and advocacy for them. He had even heard how, as faculty advisor to the Veterans Club at St. Thomas, I had sent some of the vets to the parking lot outside a school dance to clear out a gang of bikers who were harassing students leaving the dance. But the Bishop advised me to be more circumspect about publicizing events such as faculty business.

The next day he sent me an inscribed copy of a self-published collection of his essays with the title *"A College President Speaks His Mind."* I'm guessing that at least a few of his colleagues pointed out that its 40 pages were more than enough to accomplish what the title offered. But the note that accompanied his gift of the book to me suggested that I read one piece in particular, the one that seemed to recommend bowing to wisdom in the face of disagreement. Nice touch!

I'm sure some thought I was hankering for the spotlight. I wasn't.

But if light could reveal the truth, so be it. Disillusion was soon to follow. Two senior members of the theology department told me that the motive behind the administration's opposition to our program was not theological at all; it was aimed at discrediting the Chair of the department so that he could be removed from his chairmanship.

Might it not have been more Christian to move him to another position or return him to full-time teaching? Why hold hostage an entire curriculum—one important enough that parents were willing to pay the costs of private college tuition in order to provide a Catholic education? In that light it seemed that offering a more vibrant and inclusive list of courses was worth a battle. I talked it over with John McCarthy and he agreed with me.

I contacted Ed Ross, student body president, and urged him to rally the troops behind a grassroots movement to prod the administration to allow the new course listings. He offered the possibility of calling a full student strike. He made his case to the administration, and they were savvy enough to avoid new publicity reporting a student strike over theology offerings. They said they would re-study the issue. No telegram from Bishop Shannon this time. Monsignor Peters retained his position.

By now I suspect I was labeled as a trouble-maker. Since I did not have tenure, St. Thomas could simply not renew my contract for next year. No doubt they had made my Dominican superiors aware of what was going on. At no point did the Dominicans oppose me or John, verbally or in writing. But neither did they ever ask for our side of the story or offer advice or support. The lack of support was telling.

Back at the Priory things weren't going much better. I had decided to give up being an ideological punching bag. I simply couldn't win.

If the line at my confessional on Saturday was long, the older brethren decided I must be giving permission to use artificial birth control. When one of them asked me directly, I simply replied that if he wanted to know, he could come to confession, confess that he was using it, and see what I said to him.

They didn't like it either that people were calling the rectory and asking what time my Mass on Sunday would be. They wanted to hear my sermons. It was not that I was a great orator or a crowd pleaser. It was that I never gave a canned sermon, never just drew a lesson from that day's Gospel, never brought out old clichés and admonitions. I can honestly say I never preached a word that I didn't believe in strongly. People could tell that my words came with the seal of conviction and a realistic sense of human fragility.

A few weeks before the Prior asked me to preach at the special celebration dedicating the month of May to the Blessed Mother, I had a brief talk with him and I was bold enough to ask him why he and the seven other priests at Holy Rosary never went out into the neighborhood to show solidarity with the minorities and poor who lived around us. He said, "Because we have enough people coming to our door." I later asked the lay brother who answered the door how many people knocked on a typical day. He said, "One or two."

Oh Lord, let us sit in the TV room and watch re-runs of "Jeopardy." These were the same people who constantly criticized me and Fr. John.

We never got the benefit of a doubt. I remember one night when the Prior woke me up at one in the morning to tell me that I had a phone call that seemed urgent and that it was from a female. I took the call, immediately got dressed, grabbed car keys and head-ed out the door. It was probably 3 a.m. by the time I got back that morning and the Prior asked me exactly where I had been and what I had been doing. I wanted to tell him I was down by the river making love. Instead I told him that one of my students had tried to commit suicide; his girlfriend called and asked me to meet her at the hospital. That is called "ministering." I turned and walked away.

In early spring, the final hammer fell on me. The chair of the Religion department at Macalester College in the Twin Cities called me and said he had been trying to find a Catholic theologian or philosopher who would be willing to lecture and discuss the Church's opposition to artificial birth control. He said the first three priests he called turned him down. Would I accept?

The Church had not yet reached a final decision on the pill so I thought it was legitimate to discuss it openly in an academic setting.

I had been wrestling with this matter at both philosophical and pastoral levels. In my opinion, use of the pill should not be regarded as sinful. The advocates of the opposite opinion built their argument around a concept of natural law, especially as explained by St. Thomas Aquinas. While readily accepting the principle of natural law as operative, I believed that the term "natural" used in a human context took on a new meaning. Animal nature, without rational thought and determined by instinct, had only one way of doing things. At the human level, there are choices. Decisions must include principles such as the common good, familial circumstances, sexual love in marriage, and so forth. As Elie Wiesel once wrote: "The laws of the soul are more important than those of nature." The pill was not an abortion-inducing medication; it works with, not against, nature and humans have the right to make a choice. On the pastoral level, I heard the sadness of people who just could not afford another child but still wanted to be wives to their husbands. In my talk at Macalester College, I explained the official stance of the Church and my questions about it. There followed an intelligent and respectful discussion.

When word got out that a Dominican had dared to question the Church's stand (even though the Vatican's pronouncement had not yet happened) I was invited to the Chancery to meet with a representative of the Archbishop of St. Paul/Minneapolis. I notified my Dominican superiors that I had been summoned and why.

I was fairly calm as I was ushered into the Monsignor's office. We exchanged pleasantries, then he got down to business. "Father Langford, we have detailed reports that you took it upon yourself to deliver a lecture at Macalester College on the topic of the Church's opposition to artificial birth control. We can't have priests/teachers giving lectures, especially at Protestant colleges, challenging the Church's stand on important issues, of which this is one." He notified me that fellow Dominicans at Holy Rosary were certain that in the confessional I was giving penitents permission to use artificial birth control. This was evidenced by the long lines outside my confessional and the short one outside theirs. My answer was equally direct. I accepted the invitation to give the lecture because I thought it embarrassing that no one else was willing to represent the Church. As for "giving permission to use artificial birth control," I said, "If my Dominican brothers want to know, all they need to do is to come to my confessional and ask my counsel on their using it."

I knew this was a smartass answer, but patience was getting harder by the minute. I decided to make bold. I asked, "Could you, the Archbishop, or someone designated by you, spend some time with me and show me where my argument fails?" He countered," You don't get it, do you? We don't have to debate with you. We are telling you to desist or you will lose your faculties in this diocese." That meant I would not be allowed to preach, teach or hear confessions. That made it clear. Either I had to sing the system's tune or I had to get away. There would be no further debate or discussion.

I left the meeting knowing that the system would force my conformity and cost me my right to think, question, or act as if I truly believed when, in fact, I didn't. I remembered Galileo.

My passion was beaten down and it seemed like I no longer had any hope that, even in different circumstances or assignments, I would ever be able to be the priest or person I had vowed to be. So what can you do? Stay and fight harder, spin your wheels as long as you can? Or walk away and be true to who you know you are. It was not my strengths I worried about; it was my fear that I would one day just echo the safe things to say. After many prayers and talks with my friends in the Order, I decided to leave Jerome behind and return to Jim.

This was not a decision made lightly. I had invested my heart and soul and ten years of my life to the Lord and his people. How ironic that I had to contemplate giving it all up. Doubts assailed me. Was I just being stubborn? Did I think I was smarter than I really was? Was this just a result of the independence and strong will that attended my struggles with my physical handicap? Was I just a rebel without a cause?

I knew many Dominicans, including my best friends, whom I admired greatly. But all that proved to be not enough. I told myself that when my name is called on Judgment Day, I want to know it is I who am being called. I did not want to respond as a worn-down functionary who had yielded to routine and was accustomed to living without the zeal and ideals that had led me to this life in the first place.

I tried one last-ditch effort to stave off my resignation. Young people, the age of my students, were being killed daily in Vietnam. I could be with them and for them. I went to the Army recruiting office and asked to be considered as a candidate to be a chaplain in Vietnam. I was told that my physical limitations would prevent this. I argued that I was a successful athlete, but to no avail. Besides, they said I would need the written approval of my religious superior. I knew that would never happen. In retrospect, I think my desire to join the military was a latent death wish that I could die as a priest alongside the young soldiers who were being killed every day in this deeply flawed war.

Anyone who thinks that resigning the priesthood

is taking the easy way out is totally mistaken. That is a fact that I know something about.

I looked back on all the blessings I had experienced in my ten years as a Dominican: the beauty of the Divine Office being chanted, the growth of a spiritual life buttressed by the deep study the Dominicans provided, wonderful friends whose commitments matched mine. Leaving was not a victory. But neither was it a defeat. It was, however, a necessity.

—6—

Finding a Place in the World

I sent resignation letters to St. Thomas College, to the Provincial of the Dominicans in the Province of St. Albert the Great, and to the Vatican, requesting dispensation from my vows, and laicization back to being a layman. My last meal at Holy Rosary gave my critics one last shot at me. When they took it, I gave them a wordless reply with a raised middle finger. Not mature. But satisfying nonetheless.

Here I was, 30 years old, possessing three pairs of black wash pants, some tee shirts, black shoes, a couple of sweaters and a jacket. No job, no car, no place of my own to live, a stranger to the world and its ways, a disappointment to my family who had taken pride in my vocation and my work. Some thought, understandably, that I hadn't really given the priesthood a chance, that I left after three years without looking for options. There was the fact that Father Hesburgh, President of Notre Dame, looked into my work at St. Thomas and was prepared to offer me a key position in the Office of Campus Ministry at Notre Dame if I would stay in the priesthood. That was tempting; but deep down I knew that some day, at some point, I could be subject to the kinds of eroded zeal that had just rocked my soul. And, by then, I would likely be too old to start a new life.

Where was my faith in all of this? Was I a quitter? Was my decision premature? Or were some wash pants, tee shirts and shoes enough to support a will that told me what I had to do. I did not act out of fear.

Elie Wiesel said it best: "Whenever an angel says 'Be not afraid!' you'd better start worrying. A big assignment is on the way."

Leaving was not an easy decision or a nicely worn path out of the woods. I paid a heavy price; the sadness of my family, the innuendos from those who see everything through eyes searching for scandal, the absolute uncertainty about finding a job that would be fulfilling.

How do you detach from something to which and for which you had invested so much of yourself? You have to move on to what is next, but you bring your past with you. We are the cumulative experience of our decisions and hopes and efforts. Our virtues and vices are habits that we have built from repeated decisions and acts. They mark our history. "*Quod scripsi,*

scripsi"– "What I have written, I have written." But the story we write continues and its chapters likely contain surprises. As T.S. Eliot put it: "For us there is only the trying. The rest is not our business."

This was still a time when resignations from the priesthood were neither common nor without raised eyebrows as the corollary. I needed some sign to guide me. It came in the mail. It was a letter from Jack Bernard, an acquisitions editor at Doubleday in New York. He had read my Galileo book and wanted me to write a similar book on the history of tension between Science and Religion. He offered me a contract and an advance of $2,000 dollars. I hastened to sign.

Two thousand dollars seemed like a fortune to me. I bought some clothes, rented a car and headed home.

The summer I lived at home was very difficult all around. There was a constant air of sadness. I spent a lot of time sending letters to a number of colleges and universities looking for a teaching position starting in the fall. There was just not a big market for an ex-priest, no matter how educated he was in philosophy and theology or that he had published a scholarly, but readable, book on Galileo that was receiving very positive reviews. Clearly, I needed to try something else. Part of the summer was spent at the home of my sister Lois and her husband Bill Berry. They were away for a month and turned their house over to me. The privacy and solitude were wonderful. And my cooking was improving.

One day when I was talking with my mom she surprised me by saying that I needed to see what life had to offer and to have more options to find a career. She pointed out that I stood a better chance in New York than in South Bend. I agreed. Using my book advance royalties, I bought a used Datsun and still had about 800 dollars. It was enough to give New York a try. The idea of a kind of clean slate, anonymity and challenge appealed to me. I packed the Datsun, hugged everybody goodbye and hit the road.

> There is a time to join
>> a time to try
>> and a time to move on.
> Each requires us to be attentive
>> and to be brave as we seek to find
>> and follow
>> the Spirit.

As I traveled east on the toll road, I felt a liberation I had not expected. A new life lay ahead of me and I was excited to find and embrace it. I remember a symbolic moment when, after a Cadillac had sped by my Datsun, I floored it and waved as I passed him back at 90 mph. I wasn't in a hurry, but neither was I going to take a back seat without a fight.

It was evening when I drove across the George Washington Bridge into Manhatten. What a sight! My eyes teared up. Here I go.

I had done some research on the least expensive hotels in NYC and reserved a room at the Carteret, a run-down hostelry on W. 28th Street near 7th Avenue.

The amenities did not matter; I was in New York, had a cheap place to sleep and my car was parked on the street in front of the hotel.

My plan was to find a job, any job that could support me until I could find a better job. I began with the myriad publishing houses in the city. I hoped to latch on to any opening, except maybe delivering messages by bicycle. I noticed that personnel managers raised their eyebrows when I gave them my address. I rose early every morning to get the day's *New York Times* so that I could search job openings. I pounded the pavement, jostled by strangers of every stature and manner of dress, walking at a speed dictated by the crowds who carried me along at their determined pace. Cabs honked and drivers yelled at each other. I heard a multitude of languages, saw people gesturing in the streets, smelled the foods offered by street vendors, and dodged into store doorways to catch my breath or check my map.

Gone were the quiet days, the chance to think, much less to contemplate, which had been the luxuries of my past decade. Now it was June and I was alone with nine million people. Even so, it was exciting and I vowed to make it here even if I had to don the uniform of a doorman or the operator of an elevator.

The Carteret has since been completely renovated and turned into luxury apartments. But back then it was dreary and had a bad reputation. After a few days there, I began to think I was the only occupant who didn't rent her or his body to pay the rent.

I ate as frugally as I could; breakfast was coffee and a pastry at Chock Full o' Nuts. Lunch was the roast beef sandwich at the Blarney Stone. After a while, the chef there always gave me an extra helping so I could have it for dinner too. I had lived with a vow of poverty; now I lived a life of poverty. It didn't matter to me; but I needed to monitor my funds carefully until I could find work.

I will admit that as the days passed with no luck on the job front and with my funds steadily dwindling, the thought crossed my mind that leaving the safety and security of the clerical life was a mistake. I prayed extra hard when I came to the words "Lead us not into temptation." And I reminded myself of the mantra of Cubs announcer Bert Wilson: "the game is never over until the last man is out." Even though the "last man" was in the on-deck circle, I was still alive. And still had hope. Albert Camus put it perfectly: "In the depths of winter I discovered there was in me an invincible summer."

It occurred to me that I should meet Jack Bernard, my editor at Doubleday, to tell him I would not be able to work on the book he signed me to write. I called his office and arranged a meeting. When I told him my situation he said:"First, get out of the Carteret" and second, "Doubleday has an opening in the copywriting department in the Garden City office. I'll talk with them." He called and set me up with a meeting. I had to ask him what copywriters do. He told me they write ad copy and the descriptive copy for book covers, catalogs and so forth. It sounded good to me. Two days later, I donned my madras jacket and a tie, and caught the Long Island train at Grand Central Station, and headed, I prayed, into my future.

Happily, the Doubleday offices were not far from the train station. I got there well in advance of the time set for the interview. This was the first time I had made it past any personnel department screening and into an actual interview.

There were four or five people sitting around a conference table when I was ushered in. After introductions, the questions began. They started by asking about the information on my résumé and soon came to the priesthood, the reasons for my leaving, and what talents I might bring to Doubleday. They seemed very impressed that I was under contract to write a book for Doubleday. I sensed the interview was going well. After about a half hour they said they wanted to caucus and they would be back in a bit.

Three minutes later they were back. I had the sense that they had already interviewed dozens of candidates and made a pact to hire the next person in line. Happily, that was me. Don Roughan said: "We'd like you to join Doubleday. I tried not to show my excitement and still to seem self-possessed. I asked, "What is the salary?" And the response was: "You will begin at $8,000 a year."

To this day I marvel at my response. I was nearly out of money and hope, had not received any offer from any company, this was a writing job which I knew I could do and I heard myself saying, "You don't really think you can hire me for $8,000." They seemed slightly dumbfounded. They left the room again for another conference. When they came back, Don said, "We can go $8,500." I didn't take a second to reply, "Thank you. I accept." To this day I wonder where my "you can't hire me for $8000" came from. They could have said "see ya" and I'd be walking back to the train headed back to the Carteret. For a lousy $500. What was it that made me want to drive when I was in the passenger seat?

In those days, Doubleday was publishing 800 titles a year. I was to be the fourth staff member of the copywriting department, joining Ned Parkhouse, Bill Guthrie and a very quiet Asian fellow who I don't think ever shared his name with me. Our department reported to Dick O'Connor who was in charge of advertising and promotion.

His office was in the Park Avenue main office in Manhattan, so we rarely saw him.

My colleagues in copywriting conspired to welcome me by an initiation assignment ready-made for a rookie. The cookbook editor, Clara Claussen, was known to be a perfectionist who was very tough on the copywriters. So, of course, they gave me the task of producing my first copy for cover and catalog on a book titled *The Fish and Shellfish Cookbook*, under the critical eye of Clara. Knowing very little about cooking, I went over the description Clara had provided to the Editorial Committee that had approved the project in the first place. I saw my assignment as needing to be accurate but also jazz it up. When I finished the copy I sent it on to Clara. My colleagues gleefully waited for her call. When it came, I had the last laugh. She said words to the effect that it was about time a copywriter had finally understood how to present one of her books. She added, "From now on I want Jim to do all my books." Of course they started calling me Clara's love child. I didn't care. I had arrived!

Word had gotten around Doubleday that there was an ex-priest working in the copywriting department. This was really at the beginning of the exodus of priests in the wake of Vatican II, Pope John XXIII, and the conservative overreaction to all the open windows in the Vatican. So I was a curiosity. Word had reached a reporter for *Look* Magazine. He called me at Doubleday and asked whether he could meet and interview me. I said no thanks. I was not bitter, not interested in public opposition to the Church or in generalizing about the increasing number of priests leaving. He said his was not that kind of story and that at this point all he was looking for was angles to follow. I relented and said OK. He was true to his word and wrote an objective piece that settled on the unrest in the Church as reflected in the number of priests reconsidering their place in it.

Two months after the *Look* story appeared, I received a call from Jean Kennedy who identified herself as the producer of The David Susskind Show, a syndicated TV talk show devoted to intelligent discussion of important current issues and events. He was also a movie and TV producer under the aegis "Talent Associates." A brief summary of his activities reads:

In a career that spanned more than 40 years and touched Hollywood, Broadway and a nation of television viewers, Mr. Susskind was a press agent, a talent scout, an impresario and a producer of films, plays and television programs ranging from classic drama and discussion shows to entertainment spectaculars.

He put five shows on Broadway, including "Rashomon," in 1959, and made 13 films, including "Raisin in the Sun" and "Requiem for a Heavyweight" in 1961. He also won many Emmy Awards and other honors for television productions, which included "Look Homeward Angel" in 1972 and "Eleanor and Franklin" in 1976.

But it was as the earnestly combative moderator of his own talk shows—"Open End," a forum that sometimes ran for hours, which began in 1958; and of its successor, "The David Susskind Show," after 1967 —that he became best-known to American audiences.

Short, silver-haired, sincere, with a mellifluous baritone voice that sometimes rambled in its painstaking search for the right words, he interviewed thousands of guests over the years: Presidents and paupers, glittering stars and forgotten people, advocates and opponents of all kinds of controversial issues.

Often, he engaged up to a dozen guests at a time, usually divided into two or more opposing camps, and he strove with probing questions and sometimes not-too-subtle suggestions, to accentuate differences and to illuminate areas of common ground.

His subjects seemed to chronicle the issues of the times—civil rights, war, abortion, terrorism, drugs, crime, exotic life styles—and his subjects were as wide-ranging as his guests, who included Harry S. Truman, Nikita S. Khrushchev, Richard M. Nixon, Robert F. Kennedy, Vietnam veterans, a ski-masked professional killer and hosts of others.

Jean Kennedy said they were putting together a program on why priests were leaving and that they wanted to have on the panel three priests who had left and one who stayed. I declined. When she asked why, I said I'm not interested in answering questions just to inform the curious. I don't need to be asked about the dating life of an ex-priest or the like. She said, "No, we intend this to be an intelligent discussion." Reluctantly I said OK.

By now, I had gladly left the Carteret and was being graciously hosted by Dan McCarthy, brother of John McCarthy, my colleague from St. Thomas College days, and also one of the volunteers who had worked in my dad's Peace Corps group in Chile, 1961-63. While I stayed with Dan, I searched the newspapers daily, looking for an apartment I could afford. Apartment hunting was, I learned, a dog-eat-dog quest. When I couldn't find anything suitable in Manhattan, I started looking in the other burroughs. I called about one that sounded good. It was not far from the subway in Queens, 30 minutes from Manhattan and not far from the Long Island Railroad.

It was worth a look. And I liked what I saw. It was in a complex of six-story apartment buildings in Kew

Gardens, Queens. The buildings were red brick, well cared for and, best of all, rent controlled. The rental agent showed me the apartment; it was bigger than any room I'd had in the Dominicans. It had a bedroom, bathroom, living room and kitchen. It was on the top floor of the Berkeley Building. To top it off, the rent was $120.00 a month! Living here I could pay my bills and bank money even on my salary. Then came another introduction to life in the real world. The agent said there were several others interested in this apartment but that, for a proper tip, I could sign it up right now.

I am not proud of paying a bribe, but I did.

Finding basic furniture in New York is not as easy as one might think. There were no malls nearby, or big box stores, or even a grocery store. I didn't have my Datsun any more. When staying with Dan McCarthy I had always to worry about parking, obeying the alternate-side-of-the street laws, and seeing my little car grow smaller as other cars seemed to crunch it, front and back, with each day. I looked for some dealer that would buy it. The Sid Barritz Company, an outfit that picked up cars on the cheap and resold them in developing countries at a large profit, said they would relieve me of the car for $200, about 25% of what I had paid for it a year before.

There was no way I could keep it and so, that wonderful friend who had carried me to New York and graced the street in front of the Carteret was mine no longer. I imagined it as a taxi in Saudi Arabia.

My first venture on the New York subway system

was a learning experience. The train pulled up, I stepped back to allow the women to board first, the doors closed and the train left. Without me. Subsequently, I learned to adapt to the situations, like how to battle your way onto the train notwithstanding men using briefcases and women their purses as battering rams. Before long I adapted. It did not bother me to hear a guy shout: "I want everybody who looks like Hubert Humphrey to get off at the next stop." When a group of punks came through the subway cars in a menacing fashion, I would go into my twitch mode and look irrational. They never bothered me. Even they are afraid of those they can't scare.

The social psychology of subway behavior was easily observable but not readily understandable. Someone needs to study the role of reading the morning newspaper to keep from interacting with other passengers; the overt lust of some who press their bodies against the woman standing next to them on a standing-room-only ride into or out of Manhattan; or, as I witnessed one time, a person hastening to take the seat of a woman who had fainted from her seat to the floor.

There were other things that were new to me. Buying a bed, dresser, desk and kitchen table was no easy task. I had to arrange for delivery, most of which would happen when I was at work. That meant tipping the building manager for each delivery he oversaw. But it got done. I remember tacking up pictures on the walls of my place. I was 30 years old and had never done that before.

I settled in happily. Except for an experience at the local Catholic church. The celebrant decided to preach about the priests who were leaving the priesthood. He said that we were like Judas and that we yielded to devils. I don't know what devils he might have been wrestling with, but I do know that when the sermon was finished and the donation basket was passed, I decided not to contribute so much as a dime to this man so he could continue to live in the style to which he had become accustomed.

My place was mostly quiet except for a nightly, loud soliloquy that came through my floor for about an hour every night. I met the tenant a few times on the elevator. He lived alone even though it sometimes seemed he was talking to someone in his nightly lectures. I nicknamed him "The Berkeley Preacher."

Kew Gardens had gained national attention some years before when people in several apartment buildings heard the screams of a woman, looked out their windows and witnessed her rape and murder without any of them doing anything about it. I knew that New York had an attitude of non-interference, but this was an all-time low.

When I told my colleagues in Garden City that I was going to be on the Susskind Show, they offered encouragement along with a new nickname for me: "Daddy Grace."

It was November 1967 when I went to the studio at WNEW, Channel 5 to meet Mr. Susskind and tape the show in front of a live audience. David Susskind was a short, handsome, vibrant man and I liked him immediately. He gave us an entire hour to explain and explore the inchoate uprising in the Church. The show went well. Mr. Susskind took an immediate shine to me. He noticed that I gesture a lot and said, "I can't help but notice how much you gesture when you talk. Are you Jewish?" I laughed and said, "Thanks for asking, but no I'm not; I already have enough problems." He was delighted.

After the show, he stopped me and asked whether I had ever considered an acting career. He offered to audition me for parts in his movie and TV productions. As flattered as I was, that was not a direction I saw myself taking.

My brother and his family were stationed temporarily at McGuire Air Force Base in New Jersey and he accepted my invitation to come to my apartment to view the airing of the Susskind Show on November 26. We all gathered around my small television set and watched the show together. I thought it was a very good, very respectful presentation on the part of all the participants.

A couple of days later I ran into the Berkeley Preacher on the elevator. He said he had seen me on TV and could I join him for a soda and conversation. I agreed. As we were chatting I asked him whether he was married and noted that I often heard him talking to someone. "Oh," he said, "I talk a lot to my mother, over there,"pointing to the other side of the room. There was no one there. He noticed my consternation and said: "Her ashes are in that canister." My heart went out to him.

Two days after the airing of the show, I had a call from a Vice-President of Doubleday, John Delaney. He said he had been in the studio audience during the taping of the Susskind Show and that he wanted to hire me away from copywriting and offer me a job as a full acquisitions editor with an office overlooking Park Avenue. This time I was smarter than to delay this dream by haggling over salary. I said yes without hesitation.

My first trip on the elevator to the fifth floor at 277 Park Ave. was like something out of a movie. I had a brand new suit and shoes to go with a few pages of notes about authors we might pursue. I was to specialize in religious/theological books for the Doubleday Image imprint. Everyone gave me a warm welcome. My office was beyond anything I might have dreamed of. The most wonderful part of it all was that I had the opportunity to learn publishing from John Delaney, truly a publishing genius.

I called Jean Kennedy and asked her to let Mr. Susskind know what being on his show had done for me. She replied: "Good. And there is more. We are holding a bag of mail addressed to you. We were going to call you and see whether you could get your mail and be in the studio for a taping of conservative Catholics led by Jesuit Fr. Dan Lyons. I said, "Well, I lived with a whole group of people who think like Dan Lyons. I'll be there with a question or two for him."

The show went as expected. Fr. Lyons lashed out at changes in the Church and my only question to him was to the effect that since you are such a staunch defender of authority how do you explain your outspoken attack on everything this pope and Vatican Council have mandated? He twitched a bit.

After the taping, Mr. Susskind came off the set to congratulate me on my promotion at Doubleday and ask me again to consider an audition. He added, "I hear you have some mail." It turned out not to be a big bag, but it was enough. Many of the letters were just appreciation for having had the courage to make my decision. A couple were job offers, one from an executive at Standard Oil. And there were a couple of offers to date or marry me and a couple of invitations to dinner. Although I was grateful for the support, I set them aside and turned my mind back to publishing.

My first Christmas in New York was magical. Anyone who has ever watched *Miracle on 34th Street* will understand why. Christmas bells ringing, snow on the sidewalks, people in colorful scarves, the windows at Macy's and Gimbels, the tree at Rockefeller Center, a subtle softening in the pace; it was all beautiful

It was tempting to get star struck in the halls of Doubleday. Famous people were always coming and going. Among the most interesting was Arthur Haley, author of books such as *Airport*, *Hotel*, and ten or eleven others. His books have sold more than 170 million copies in 40 languages. He told me that when he was starting out and being deluged with rejection slips, his family believed in him. His children delivered newspapers and his wife worked full time to keep the mortgage paid and food on the table. With faith like that, you can indeed move mountains.

And there was Bill Barrett, author of *Lilies of the Field* with a similar story. There were many that you just saw at a distance: Audrey Hepburn, Robert Kennedy, Bill Moyers, and so on. My point is not to namedrop, but simply to say that it was nice to lay eyes on people who made a difference in our world.

My first full year in New York had brought incredible surprises and much joy. That first winter, Austine Noonan—easily the most beautiful young lady working at Doubleday, invited me to go with her and a group of friends for a weekend ski trip to Stratton Mountain, Vermont. I said that it sounds life fun, but I don't know how to ski. She said come anyway, you'll have a great time. I went.

What happened there became a memory I can still picture as if it is happening right now. It has nothing to do with Austine.

I had skis on and was trying to walk or slide with them at the foot of the mountain when suddenly a couple of skiers, finishing their run, pulled up right beside me. I stood there being greeted by Bobby and Ethel Kennedy. We said hello and laughed about the cold, and then they were gone. The next time I would see him was as he lay in state at St. Patrick's Cathedral in New York. I was humbled to have crossed lives ever so briefly with such a couple.

A friend of one of my students at St. Thomas had stayed in touch with me by occasional letters and phone calls. She was bright, nice looking, the survivor of a somewhat tough upbringing. She stood in contrast to some of the women I met in New York. I began to be attracted to her in some kind of ideal way. And I think she fell in love with the whole concept of falling for someone who seemed to have at least some possession of goodness. We both succumbed to something of an impossible ideal. In time, I bought a ring, took her to Central Park and proposed. She said yes.

It was not as simple as most marriages. I wanted to be married in the Church and that required that the Vatican act on the petition I had sent more than a year before. One day I received a request to come to the Chancery in Brooklyn to discuss my petition. I was taken in to what seemed like a small courtroom. A priest came in, said that he had been designated by the Vatican to ask me some questions and forward my responses to Rome. My mind flashed back to Galileo who, when questioned by the Inquisitor, was faced with the words: "Do you know why we called you here?" I told the good father that I had waited a year to hear back from Rome and that I had gone through all the steps required to obtain laicization. He said he would get right on it.

After the papers came back with the instruction that had to be kept secret (oh Lord, we wouldn't want anyone to know that a priest can obtain laicization), we were free to be married in the chapel of the Chancery in Brooklyn.

It was not to be a marriage made in heaven. Disillusion set in on both of us fairly early. But we both gave it our best try for most of the ten years we stayed together. And it yielded two very wonderful sons. Eventually, the marriage was annulled, meaning it had not been a marriage at all.

My second year at Doubleday began to yield some results. I signed up and published Christopher Mooney's wonderful book on Teilhard de Chardin, arranged for a paperback edition of the first two volumes of the new translation of the *Summa Theologica*, and signed five other projects that turned out well for the authors and Doubleday. I learned how to meet the market by watching John Delaney with his uncanny sense of when and where to turn next.

Early in 1969, I began to think about getting back into an academic setting. I wanted time and opportunity to research the book I was contracted to write for Doubleday. But I didn't want to give up publishing. Then one day, paging through the openings listed in the back of *Publishers Weekly*, I came across a listing for the Executive Editor position at the University of Michigan Press in Ann Arbor. I knew Michigan to be a great university, especially in graduate studies. Their faculty was superior and their Law School one of the three best in the country.

It wasn't that I thought that two years in publishing would qualify me for the job, but I decided to respond to the ad, send a résumé and a cover letter asking how much more experience I would need before I could qualify for a job like this. I was looking for information and advice. I was surprised a week later when a call came from the Director of the Michigan Press, Glenn Gosling. He informed me that his chief editor and Associate Director, Scott Mabon, had in fact just purchased the right to publish my Galileo book as an Ann Arbor Paperback. That put my work in great company...Erasmus, Aristotle, Duckett, Waddel, Michelet, and many more. I was thrilled. Then Mr. Gosling said he would be in New York City the next week and would like me to join him at the bar of the Roosevelt Hotel, which happened to be just down the street from my office. I said I'd be delighted. It would be my chance to pick his brain about what I needed to do to qualify for university press publishing.

I was excited to meet Mr. Gosling. He was a tall, thin, nice person.

We ordered a drink and I asked him about the Michigan Press. He said that his Executive Editor had left for a Vice Presidency at Cambridge University Press. He had himself begun his career at Henry Holt in New York and his claim to fame was his signing of Audie Murphy's bestseller, and later movie, *To Hell and Back*. So he himself had gone directly from trade publishing to university press publishing. In logic, you can always argue from the fact to the possibility. We had another cocktail. Was this conversation going the way it seemed? He explained the differences between university presses and trade publishers and made a point of saying that my Galileo book was certainly evidence that I could handle the intellectual part of the position.

He said, "I like talking with you. I like you. I want

to fly you to Ann Arbor to take a look at the Press and the University and meet our staff." He added, "I'll call you with particulars. We will, of course, pay all expenses and put you up at the Michigan Union, the place where, in March of 1960, candidate for president, John F. Kennedy, announced the idea of a Peace Corps.

We decided to have another drink to celebrate.

I thanked him and bade him a safe trip home. And then it dawned on me...he looked a little like that third drink had taken a toll. As I left, I had the distinct feeling that he would forget our discussion and that I'd never see him again.

But fate, or Divine Providence, or both, had it in mind that I was going to Ann Arbor. Mr. Gosling did indeed call with an invitation.

The flight was into Detroit; then a 40-mile limo trip to Ann Arbor ensued. Even though I had grown up in Indiana, just 10 miles south of the Michigan state line, I was not prepared for the habits of Michigan drivers. They must have taken Drivers Ed in Mexico City or on the Autobahn in Germany. I had read enough Camus to know the elements of absurdity...like being killed on your way to the future you have always dreamed of.

The introductions and interview highlighted a splendid day in Ann Arbor. It is a great city and the University seems to fit it well.

However, one could sense a growing tension that accompanied the frequent and increasingly intense demonstrations against the Vietnam War. Along with University of California at Berkeley and Columbia

University, the University of Michigan was a hotbed of political unrest.

Although I was sad to leave my friends at Doubleday and grateful to have been a small part of a great team as I learned the business, I was thrilled to be going back to the Midwest and becoming Executive Editor of a widely respected university press. The offer was made, including a 50% salary increase, excellent benefits and access to U of M Hospital for medical care. It had been there, more than three decades before, that my birth stroke had been correctly diagnosed.

Moving was easy. We didn't have much to move and the Press was footing all the costs. At the other end, an old friend, Art Wiggins, arranged temporary housing for us until we could settle in and look for a home of our own. We piled into our Volkswagen Beetle and headed west. There have been many times in the years since then that I miss New York City and, as I write this, my memory flashes pictures of the Carteret, the Long Island Railroad, subways, the Berkeley Preacher, David Susskind, Park Avenue, the Village, friends like John Ware, Jeff Warner, Pat Kossman, Mike Leach (also a former priest), and the colorful sidewalks of Manhattan packed with people of every type and size.

I can't imagine there is any place like it in the world. It has a permanent place in my heart.

—7—

No Time to Rest

As with any new job, the first thing to do is to report to Human Resources, fill out numerous forms, and get at least partially acclimated to the surroundings. The University of Michigan is a large enterprise: more than 38,000 students, 6,000 faculty and 8,000 staff and maintenance people. The University is typically ranked among the top universities in the U.S. The campus is incorporated into the city of Ann Arbor. It has wonderful shops, restaurants and coffee places. It bustles, but not in the way New York does.

The atmosphere was electric. This is where, in 1964, a group of faculty held the nation's first "teach in" against U.S. Policy in Southeast Asia. This is where the Students for a Democratic Society was founded and grew quickly. Shortly before we got to Ann Arbor,

20,000 rallied in Michigan Stadium to protest the war. Large gatherings, students mostly, could be found almost anywhere on or around campus. Graffiti decorated the walls and buildings. I remember a large sign painted on the brick wall of the building next to the Press that pleaded "Free Martin Sostre." I simply assumed that he was some local figure who had been jailed. In actuality, he was a well-known radical who had been imprisoned at Attica on trumped-up charges.

Sometimes the crowd got really worked up and the Washtenaw Sheriff's troops were called in. Usually that made things worse and established a very strong antipathy beween the two sides. Reports circulated about how students who were arrested were treated in the local jail. Escalation was just a matter of time.

University President Robben Fleming did an amazing job helping to prevent violent outbreaks and he did so by meeting with the SDS and other groups rather than condemning them.

Ever since I had helped bury a student I had taught the year before at St. Thomas and who came home from Vietnam in a casket, I had become increasingly against the war. Our intervention in Vietnam seemed to be built on a domino theory positing that if Vietnam fell, all of Southeast Asia would soon follow.

A draft was put into place; if you were young, male, and unable to claim connections that could mark you as exempt from the draft, you were subject to a kind of lottery and a call to the military. Minorities, the poor, those who could not get a college exemption, were especially vulnerable to the draft. Students began to burn their draft cards, some left for haven in Canada. All over the country there were massive demonstrations urging power for the people, the end to war and justice for all. Institutions that were symbols of the system were targeted for broken windows and more. Picketing led to blocking and arrests, which led to more protests and more arrests. In short, this was not a quiet little town in the Midwest. More than once as I left the press building, I was met by bayonet-bearing rifles in the hands of national guardsmen.

The university press was located at 615 E. University, less than a stone's throw from the main quad and the center of campus. My office, though not really large, was more than adequate. I studied the backlist and current schedule of books at the press and researched the works in progress and the professional interests of the faculty. In the library I spent my time scanning journals in the fields in which I was knowledgeable. It was not long before I contacted and met faculty who were working on interesting projects. Word of mouth started bringing calls to me from faculty who heard that I was shaking the bushes looking for good manuscripts.

I liked the people at the press, especially John Scott Mabon, Nancy Sandweiss, Tom Nicely, Terry Zak, Mary Irwin, and Bob Weiss. The process of getting a project approved was to clear it with Scott Mabon and Glenn, and then present it, along with critical reviews by scholars, to the faculty editorial board.

Among the first persons I met was Nicholas

Steneck, a rising star in medieval studies and also the history of science. After hearing my background, he asked me if I would be interested in teaching a course in the new concentration he was founding, the Medieval Collegium. I assured him that if I could get permission from the Director of the Press, I'd love to create a course on themes of medieval philosophy. Permission was granted. Glenn Gosling thought it would be advantageous to have his Executive Editor on the teaching faculty. I would be glad to be back in the classroom, so it would work out well for all concerned.

Early on, I made many friends among the faculty, notably Anatol Rapoport, Don Warren, Eric Rabkin, Bill Porter, Bill Haney, Leonard Greenbaum, and Austin Warren. I met the deans of the colleges and Law School and asked them for tips on projects being developed in their domains.

As soon as finances allowed, we looked for a house to buy. We found it. The house was a two-story frame building at 1317 Pontiac Trail. It had been built in 1836 by William Perry who operated a bookstore nearby. Soon after, it was acquired by Josiah Beckley who, with his brother, Guy, was an avid abolitionist. It was common knowledge that the Beckleys were part of the Underground Railroad and that they helped fugitive slaves who were on their way to Canada, avoid slave hunters and sheriffs' deputies. There had been a hiding place in the back of a downstairs closet large enough for three or four people to hide when necessary.

The house was in very good shape; there was a

small barn in back on the oversized lot. The basement walls were built of large rocks and mortar. The first floor had back-to-back fireplaces. The second floor was bedrooms and bath. Had there been any ghosts haunting that house, they would have been good ones.

An old house, restrictive budget and personal preference brought me into the world of antique shopping, refinishing and furnishing. I met a dealer with a large shop only blocks away who became a good friend. Al Crist was a pleasant, knowledgeable and honest man who introduced me into his world of smart buying, fixing and selling antiques. Oak pieces were plentiful, as were pine and, less so, walnut. As family farms faded, auctions and moving sales were plentiful and the prices were right. Al taught me about restoring and refinishing furniture. It became a passion.

As the summer of 1969 yielded to the fall, another passion of mine took a hit. My Cubs, who had not won a world series since 1908, had held first place in the National League from opening day until September 10, when the hated New York Mets replaced them and went on to be world champions. It broke my heart. I blamed the manager, Leo Durocher, who played the regulars day-in and day-out until they just ran out of energy. The day would come, ten years later, when I would tell the whole story in a book.

In the spring of 1970, the protests began to expand dramatically, both in frequency and in the issues being challenged. We had Black Panthers, White Panthers and Gray Panthers all agreeing on pushing against the war, but also for civil rights and justice here at home. The Black Action Movement was born and successfully supported their list of demands for more admissions, scholarships and equal status, by instigating a campus-wide strike that blocked campus buildings and the daily life of the University. It ended only when the administration agreed to many of BAM's demands.

Students also lobbied the City Council to pass an ordinance that decriminalized marijuana and made its possession a misdemeanor punishable by a fine of five dollars.

Though not closely, I was involved with some student groups as a kind of advisor. The spirit and passion of this generation made me confident that better days lay ahead. And I attended some of the rallies. I remember one where students were excited that cameras were clicking away rapidly on the crowd. The students thought their pictures would be in the newspaper. I suggested that it was more likely that they would be filed in a field office of the FBI. Federal presence increased and it was noted that the CIA had operatives keeping tabs on the Panther groups, the SDS and others. The two or three times I wrote letters to the editor that appeared in the *Ann Arbor News* netted me several phone calls, one threatening my life.

That same year, 1970, marked the birth of Jeremy William Langford. We had gone through the Lamaze training and prepared for natural childbirth. Labor took hours and hours but finally Jeremy came into the world at the University of Michigan Hospital.

His mother was quintessentially good at nurturing him. Our love for him was one of the few things we shared and, at that point, she was better at it than I was. Jeremy was baptized in the chapel of the Newman Center in Ann Arbor. Seventeen months later, his brother, Joshua McCarty Langford also was born at the University Hospital and it is a good thing I was there. Second babies often come out more quickly than first babies. Dr. Jeffries was in the hall when I could see Joshua ready to emerge. I clearly was not going to hold him back. So I caught him. *Deo Gratias*!

My work at the Press was yielding good results. I first took note of Law Professor Arthur R. Miller by reading his article in the *Michigan Law Review*. He was onto a hot-button issue, namely the invasion of personal privacy by the government. I called him and arranged a meeting. It was the beginning of a collaboration and friendship. He liked the idea of expanding his article into a more comprehensive look at the way computers and data banks were being used to keep records on citizens. We met often as he developed chapters. It became clear to me that this would be a ground-breaking book with the potential for media attention and sales. As I re-read his book today, I am amazed by how his concerns and predictions made 45 years ago have come to pass. The book, *The Assault on Privacy: Computers, Data Banks, and Dossiers*, was an instant success. It did not hurt that endorsements came in from Senators Sam Ervin and Hubert Humphrey, as well as consumer advocate Ralph Nader. A large book club adopted it as a main selection, the *Today Show* booked Professor Miller and the *New York Times* published a strong review. Sadly for me, before long, the Harvard Law School came calling and left with a commitment from Arthur to join their faculty.

Sales were good enough to enable us to publish more scholarly books we otherwise could not have afforded. I brought in plenty of scholarly books that aimed to advance knowledge in various fields, but also books on the power structure in Black neighborhoods, a book titled *The Radical Center*, predictive of political attitudes still very much in play, *The Neighborhood Organizer's Handbook, and Assault on the Media: The Nixon Years*. I signed up *Compromising the Constitution* by Rexford Tugwell who had been a young member of FDR's Brains Trust.

Probably the most interesting drama unfolded when I received a call from Bill Porter, Chair of the Journalism Department at U of M. He raved about a manuscript written by a sophomore about her summer project interviewing and describing how the political reaction to the war in Vietnam had divided the people of Watertown, Wisconsin. Bill said it was very powerful and that I should take a look. I read it and really wanted to publish it. Mr. Gosling said if I wanted to take it to the Editorial Board, he would allow me to do so but would not support or oppose it.

The editorial board on university presses were senior scholars from various departments assigned to make sure that everything they approved would carry the seal of the university proudly. How could they possibly allow a book by a sophomore? I showed them outside reviews that praised the work and added that I would be happy to put my job on the line with this book. It was very much needed to exemplify how the war was dividing our country. I reminded the board that they were there to protect the imprint based on the contents and style of the project, not to vote based on the academic rank of the authors. I said if they turned it down, I would consider taking it and myself to another press. Reluctantly, they approved it. And so *Crisis in Watertown: The Polarization of an American Community*, by Lynn Eden was published. It was the right time for such a book and Lynn was the right author for it. Bill Porter and I were vindicated when this book by a 19-year-old finished second to *Fire in the Lake* by Frances Fitzgerald in the competition for the National Book Award.

On the more scholarly end of the spectrum, I was able to publish my old mentor, Father Weisheipl's *The Development of Physical Theory in the Middle Ages*, a two-volume work on *Causality and Scientific Explanation* by William Wallace, *Galileo Studies* by Stillman Drake of the University of Toronto, and *Connections* by Austin Warren, a well-respected literary critic.

I truly enjoyed my work at Michigan. But when Mr. Gosling was removed as Director of the Press and Scott Mabon was bypassed in the ensuing search for his replacement, I began to think about applying for a directorship at some other university press. My reasoning was simple: I wanted to see whether my ideas and approach would work in an operation where I could implement them without so much spinning of wheels. I was determined to find a position where there would not be a repeat of the peacock-like denial of a book I presented for approval. It was by Harvey Wheeler, author of *Fail Safe*, which had been made in to a successful movie. One member of our board didn't like Wheeler's politics and garnered enough support to kill the present project. My philosophy was and is, if a book is well researched, well argued and well written, it doesn't matter whether it is Catholic, Protestant, Jewish or Muslim, Democratic or Republican in tone, it should be published.

When Joshua was born in 1972, it became clear that we needed a larger house and one away from the traffic noises on Pontiac Trail. We put that wonderful old house up for sale and bought a ranch house and land at 2185 Ayrshire Road, off of Plymouth Rd. It was my first encounter with well and septic systems and country living. When it became clear that the land was too much clay even to plant a vegetable garden, I decided to build a clay tennis court in the back area. Bulldozers, fence builders, a heavy-duty roller, and net posts became the order of the day.

When it was completed, I called my dad and urged him to bring mom and come to see the court. My friend Art Wiggins and I had some good battles on that court.

A year and a half later I was combing the job

vacancies on the back pages of *Publisher's Weekly*. Before I could even identify a target, I had a call from a publishing friend, Emily Schossberger, Director of the University of Notre Dame Press. She said she was retiring and wondered whether I would be interested in applying to be her successor. Talk about the right place and the right time! She gave me particulars and urged me to get my hat in the ring as soon as I could.

I thought it was at least a minor miracle. Imagine. Notre Dame. My philosophy and theology degrees and publishing experience, now up to seven years, and my love for that University put it at the top of my dream list.

I put a résumé together, listed the books I had signed and supplied the names of references I hoped the search committee would contact. I learned later that John Delaney and Ken McCormick from Doubleday, as well as Scott Mabon, Arthur Miller and Bill Porter from Michigan all provided strong recommendations. But one of the search committee members told me later that the strongest and most unusual recommendations came from Walter Sears who had just replaced Glen Gosling at U of M Press. He wrote: "I just became Director here. I am counting on Jim Langford to be my right hand. Keep your cotton-picking hands off of him."

A week or so later I received a call inviting me to Notre Dame for an interview. If I recall correctly, there were four or five people on the search committee and the only one I knew was Dick Conklin who had been at St. Thomas College when I was there. The interview went well. I was informed that there were more than 70 applications and that the committee would select four finalists from that list. It was nearly two weeks later when they named me as one of the finalists and invited me for another interview, this time with a representative of the Provost, a chief financial officer, and the Dean of the Graduate School. Before the interview I dropped by to say hello to my longtime friend, Father Jerome Wilson, a Vice President of the University.

He said that I should think twice before accepting the job if offered.

He pointed out that the finances of the Press, the fact that it lost money annually, left it in jeopardy. If the losses continued, the University might decide to discontinue the Press. I said that almost all of the 70 U.S. university presses lost money, but the parent universities supported them as part of being a responsible institution of higher education. And, I pointed out, Notre Dame Press had the potential to become the largest and best Catholic university press in the world. He smiled and wished me the best.

The interview went well. When they asked what I thought of the idea that the Press should be moved from the jurisdiction of the Provost to the Business Office I said that would be a big mistake. Its excellence would not be as a profit-making venture, but as an academic one. The Provost should oversee the Press and I let them know I felt strongly about that.

It was approximately ten days later that I received

a call from the secretary to Father James Burtchaell, Provost. She said that Fr. Burtchaell had a couple of hours between planes at O'Hare Airport in Chicago in a few days and could I arrange to meet him there. She seemed a little taken aback when I said no. People normally did not say no to him. He had earned a reputation as a tough and demanding administrator.

He was brilliant, had studied at Cambridge in the UK, and his standards were relentlessly high. People feared him because he believed that the laissez faire atmosphere of years past needed to be challenged. As one professor put it, he was doing the unpopular task of clearing out the deadwood.

His secretary replied that Father would be traveling for the next two weeks. I said, assuming that this is about the job, I don't do business between planes at an airport. I could wait to see him until he returned to campus. In retrospect, I think he liked...or at least respected...my answer. In a way it was reminiscent of my moment at Doubleday when I refused their first offer.

When our meeting finally took place, we had a frank discussion about what he hoped and I believed the Press would accomplish. Echoing Father Wilson, he said he could offer me a five-year contract, matching the time the financial people were willing to grant to see whether the Press could be turned around and at least cut back on its losses. I left his office impressed with him and confident that if we delivered, he would be our staunchest ally. We agreed on a salary and I went to the Personnel office to fill out forms. In those days, a formal contract was not necessary. Fred Freeman, Director of Personnel, and I shook hands and that was it.

Back in Ann Arbor it was time to sell the house and to make some trips to South Bend in search of a home to buy. We found it quickly. It was a tan brick, two story, nicely designed and well-maintained home at 109 Napoleon Blvd. It was in the Harter Heights neighborhood, only a half-mile from Otsego St. where I had lived for two years of high school and my year at Notre Dame, and a few blocks from where my sister Lois and her husband Bill Berry lived. If I remember correctly, we agreed to $32,500 as the purchase price.

It didn't take long for us to sell the house in Ann Arbor. Notre Dame paid the moving expenses so that part was easy. It was time to go home.

I was thrilled to be back at Notre Dame and eager to use my skills to build a major-league press.

At that time, the Press was located on the fifth floor of the Hesburgh Memorial Library (the building with the touchdown Jesus mural on it). I had reserved the right to hire and fire as needed in order to insure a team I could lead and who would be willing to work with me. I interviewed everybody on the staff and chose all but one of them to stay. Soon we hosted an open house so that interested faculty could come by and get a sense of what we were about.

Father Burtchaell and I had agreed that for my first year I would work with the existing faculty board and that henceforth I would submit a list of three names from which to select two new members of the board who completed their two-year terms.

I continued to stay in touch with some of my authors from Michigan. Don Warren, Frithjof Bergmann, Bill Frankena, William Wallace and Nick Steneck, among others, brought their projects to Notre Dame and, by so doing, immediately increased the range of our list. Learning the Notre Dame faculty alerted me to a number of significant leads that I hoped to turn into books for our program. A university press does not exist to publish only works by local faculty. The goal is to develop strengths that will draw scholars from other universities who are attracted by the excellence of your program in their area. I wanted the best books from our faculty in areas where we were or wanted to be outstanding such as Philosophy, Ethics, Literature, Catholic History and Latin American Studies. But I also wanted to attract the best scholars from elsewhere by enticing them to publish with Notre Dame.

One of my first moves was also one of my best. I heard that a young member of the American Studies faculty was working on a book to be titled *The University of Notre Dame: A Portrait of Its History and Campus.* The only real history of Notre Dame at the time was *Notre Dame One Hundred Years,* which covered 1842-1942 and was published in 1948. The author, Fr. Arthur J. Hope, may have missed some facts but he wrote with a flourish. Schlereth told the story of the place but, more importantly, he uncovered, discovered and collected photographs that captured Notre

Dame history. I signed the project without hesitation. It was published in 1976 and sold well enough that, with a few other new titles moving quickly, the Press was now on solid footing in the second year of my tenure. The problem that created was what to do with the profits.

Father Edmund P. Joyce, Executive Vice President of the University felt that any surplus funds should revert to the University and be added to the general funds. I appealed to Fr. Burtchaell who agreed with me that the extra money should be used to fuel growth of the Press. After what must have been a bit of a battle between these two administrators, the decision was made that the Press could retain half of its profits. Well, it was better than nothing.

Remaking the Press took more hours than the nine-to- five routine and I frequently had to go back to my office after dinner and bedtime for the kids. That became a cause of tension. And there was an unusual social situation. We were invited to parties at faculty homes, but soon learned to say no thanks more often than yes. In part, this was because all too often I was buttonholed by someone trying to sell me on publishing his or her manuscript. It was like a bus man's holiday spent riding on Greyhound. A second issue was that I wanted to avoid the criticism aimed at my predecessor who published numerous books by her numerous friends. I did not want to give even a hint of possible favoritism. This did not mean that I lacked friends, but only that people could not easily identify me as a member of this or that social group. That same philosophy applied to my relationship to the Press staff. I did not play favorites.

Part of my editorial development plan was to go back to Ann Arbor occasionally to see friends and recruit authors. In short order some great projects came from Michigan to Notre Dame. These included *Perspectives on Morality* by William Frankena, one of the foremost authorities in philosophical ethics. Frithjof Bergmann, one of the great teachers at Michigan brought us his masterpiece, *On Being Free*. Donald Warren who had published two books with me at Michigan, one on the dynamics of Black Neighborhoods and one on the development of what he called *The Radical Center* in American politics, brought us *The Neighborhood Organizer's Handbook*, and Nick Steneck committed to Notre Dame his excellent study *Science and Creation in the Middle Ages*. Breakthroughs started to happen more frequently. We signed up a young theologian named Stanley Hauerwas who would go on to publish four books with us as he gained widespread national attention for his work in Ethics. Stanley liked how we published his books and he talked us up to colleagues from other universities. That is how the word gets out. But you need also to sign the stars from your own campus, people like Julian Samora in Latino Studies, John Dunne, Lawrence Hoffman in Theology, David Burrell and Ernan McMullin in Philosophy Stephen Kertesz and Matthew Fitzsimons in Political Studies, Jay P. Dolan and Fr. Tom Blantz in Catholic History. We did that.

Nor did we avoid studies that might be controversial. In 1977, we published *The Politics of Population Control* by Tom Littlewood, written during his fellowship at the Institute of Politics at Harvard. It had several chapters on political pressure applied by American bishops working to guide public policy on population. Tom noted in his Introduction,

> The role that the Catholic church plays in the scenes that follow is less than a heroic one. But Jim Langford, Director of the University of Notre Dame Press, encouraged my project and assisted me at every step of the way. The spirit of free discussion is alive and well at Notre Dame, and I am grateful.

There were two occasions in my 25 years at Notre Dame Press when free speech became an issue. The first happened in 1981 when we published a book titled *Power and Authority in the Catholic Church: Cardinal Cody in Chicago*, a revised doctoral dissertation at the University of Wisconsin by Charles Dahm, O.P. When the local Bishop of the Fort Wayne-South Bend diocese got wind of it, he rushed to Corby Hall, the center of the Holy Cross priests at Notre Dame, and expressed his strong disapproval of the book; he wanted the presses stopped. He hadn't even read the book.

When I learned that the Bishop was on the warpath, I sent a note to Father Hesburgh and stood by the book. At the same time, I told him that I didn't want to be the cause of a rift between the Bishop and Notre Dame. I offered to resign. In the afternoon campus mail that day came a response from Father Ted. It was my resignation torn into bits and a note that said: "We do not punish people at Notre Dame for responsible use of free speech."

The second occasion for defending free speech came a few years later. The bishop sent a letter saying he was distressed to discover that books published by the University Press on matters of theology or ethics did not carry an Imprimatur from him guaranteeing the orthodoxy of the contents. I pointed out that every book we publish in those fields has gone through two scholarly reviews. In addition, for us to print an Imprimatur would be an embarrassment in the academic world and confirm the view of some scholars that Notre Dame Press was just a mouthpiece for the Church. I called a staff meeting and asked how it was that he was obtaining our books. Surely he wasn't haunting the local Waldens waiting to see the latest title from Notre Dame. Our publicity manager solved the issue: the Bishop was on our complimentary list for every book we publish. I said "Take him off the list." She did and we never heard from him again.

One of the best strategic moves I made early in my tenure at Notre Dame Press was in 1978 when I met with Professor Alan Olsen of Boston University. He described a series they were inaugurating at the Institute for Philosophy and Religion at Boston University. The idea was to select a topic of importance and invite some of the best thinkers in the world to address the topic in an original piece to be delivered in a public and broadcast lecture at BU and subsequently to be honed and submitted for a book. Each year would sur-round a different topic.

Most publishers, including me, were leery of any collection of essays. Libraries tended to avoid collec-tions of essays resulting from a meeting or colloquium. But this was different. The publisher would be involved in selecting the topic and the manuscript would come already carefully edited and often revised. When Alan told me the list of invitees they had in mind for the first two volumes, I knew I wanted this series to carry the logo of Notre Dame Press.

Later that year, the general editor of the series flew out to meet me and negotiate an agreement. He was Leroy S. Rouner, Professor of Philosophy and Direc-tor of the Institute for Philosophy and Religion at B.U. Over lunch at the Morris Inn, Leroy told me about his life and family. He choked up when he started talking about his son Tim who had died in a mountain climb-ing accident a year before. The story was so moving that I had tears too. He rapidly became one of the best friends I have had in all my life.

The inaugural and subsequent 22 volumes in this series are a veritable who's who of the world's greatest thinkers reflecting on topics such as courage, human rights and the world's religions, death and dying, the foundations of ethics, civility, friendship, happiness and so on. The series brought Notre Dame Press into direct contact with this stellar group of authors and we were able to publish other books by Elie Wiesel, Herb Mason, Alasdair MacIntyre, Jürgen Moltmann, and the like.

The books by Alasdair MacIntyre have an interesting history. He is a brilliant man and I heard he would be giving a lecture on campus. I attended and was absolutely impressed with his thesis and presentation. I went up to talk with him after the lecture and said that if this piece was to be part of a book, I'd like to publish it. He said that the book was already under contract to Harper and Row. I replied that if, for any reason, that did not work out, I'd take it on the spot. Some months later, he called me to say that Harper thought the book was "too academic" and they asked to terminate the contract. I said immediately, "I'll take it."

To abridge the story, that book, titled *After Virtue: A Study in Moral Theory* became the best seller in the history of the Press. Published in 1981, it has sold over 100,000 copies. That was the beginning of a friendship and our working together to bring back into print three of his earlier titles and publishing two more new ones. I venture to say that the Harper editor who turned down *After Virtue* has his portrait hanging in the restroom at Harper.

On the domestic front, I got involved in a neighborhood zoning controversy. We lived at 109 Napoleon St. which was located in the Harter Heights neighborhood, not far from Notre Dame. Since it was traditionally for single families, a number of homeowners became concerned when a growing list of houses were taken over by absentee landlords who were renting them to four, five or six students at a time. Were that to continue, the whole area would change from a nice place to raise children into a college congery with negative results for quiet, safety and property values. After several meetings, the homeowners decided to follow the lawful route to save the area.

There was at the time a Catholic Charismatic group, the People of Praise, who were establishing group homes for its members. Some of these homes were within Harter Heights. Their leaders decided that our effort to seek single family zoning was aimed at them. Although it clearly affected their plans, we were not aiming at them.

They decided to go on the attack. Their members were told that our attorney, Bob Konopa, and I were "doing the work of the devil" and they door knocked through the neighborhood with that message. Having been called Judas from the pulpit in New York, I think I preferred that to being accused of working for the devil.

An overflow crowd turned out for the Area Plan Commission hearing on the issue; the majority were members of the People of Praise. A number of them spoke about how they had been "saved" in their households and what evils would occur if they were stopped from acquiring more properties in Harter Heights. The Area Plan Commission decided not to rule for or against the Harter Heights proposal. I guess the potato was too hot for them to handle. That meant it would go to the City Council for a decision.

Before that happened, I delved more into who these people were. One young woman told me that her daughter had epilepsy and that the leader of her household had instructed her to take the child off of her medications. Instead, the community would lay hands on the child, pray for her and she would be healed. I spoke to the head of the People of Praise and told him that while we were not opposed to them per se, our aim was to save a whole section of the city, and that households like his could easily fit in multiple family zones. I also mentioned that I now knew enough to speak to the Council about his organization itself and reveal its strange goings on. The City Council meeting was jammed. The debate was heard. Harter Heights won. A neighborhood was saved.

In 1979, Father Burtchaell stepped down as Provost in favor of a very bright mathematics professor, Timothy O'Meara. As might be expected, this change brought with it apprehension as to what kind of priority he might give to the Press. We had never published in mathematics and had no intention of doing so. What Provost O'Meara did have working for him was a clear vision of what needed to be done to move the University toward becoming a full-scale research university. That was going to require much greater resources to pay for facilities, the salaries of recognized scholars, graduate student scholarships, housing and library resources.

Tim O'Meara deserves great credit for his dedication to advancing scholarship during his tenure as Provost. When he stepped down, he was replaced by Nathan Hatch, who continued O'Meara's pursuit of excellence. When Hatch resigned in 2005, the new Provost was Thomas Burish who left the Presidency at Washington and Lee University to come home to Notre Dame. I am still amazed by his masterful work as Master of Ceremonies when President Barack Obama spoke at graduation in 2009.

One change that happened quickly under O'Meara was that the Press was moved out of the Hesburgh Library and relegated to a share of the maintenance building, just south of the university transportation center and gas pumps. I suggested that we redesign our logo and incorporate the gas pumps, but the staff recommended restraint. The move did not leave a lot of doubt as to our position on the roster of important arms of the administration. We made the best of it. There were new centers springing up all over campus as having a center seemed to be necessary to apply for and obtain grants for specific programs. Finally a use for the redesigned logo! I asked our designer to produce a logo for what I named "The Center for Creative Publishing." Of course it included the gas pumps. We hung it on the door of the janitor's closet. The janitor seemed to like it. So did we. Years later, thanks to then President "Monk" Malloy, the Press was moved from the maintenance building to half an entire floor in Flanner Hall. We seemed finally to have come of age!

In 1977, Father Hesburgh was appointed to President Gerald Ford's committee for reconciliation after Vietnam. He wanted a study to be undertaken and the results published in a book as soon as possible.

He hoped to have it on the desk of every senator and member of the House before the first session of the New Year began. The purpose of the committee was to make recommendations with regard to draft or military offenders during the Vietnam years. I told Father that, even with priority, it would take eight or nine months to produce a book once we had the manuscript. And I followed that by saying we will pull out all the stops and have books in 12 weeks.

The policy recommended in the book is the one adopted by President Ford and Congress. Hundreds of young people were reconciled with their country.

It was also in 1977 that I first met Elie Wiesel. He had been invited to give the Ward-Phillips Lectures, a series of four talks in four evenings, around the topic the chosen lecturer would designate.

I knew him only vaguely as the author of *Night* one of the most moving books of the twentieth century. Professor Wiesel had survived Auschwitz and Buchenwald, but his mother and father and a sister had not. He had been a boy of 14 when the Nazis came to his village of Sighet and taken away all of the Jews. He was deeply versed in Jewish history and tradition. He was a hasid and his lectures at Notre Dame would be titled *Four Hasidic Masters and Their Struggle against Melancholy*. One of the stipulations in the Ward-Phillips contract required the speaker to provide a manuscript based on the lectures for publication by the Press.

Like most of the students and others, I was not familiar with the Hasidic movement in eastern Europe.

But I had to attend the lectures. Something really amazing ensued. Elie Wiesel's opening talk mesmerized all of us in attendance. He was so eloquent and in such a quiet delivery that no one there wanted to leave when it was over. Word spread quickly. The next evening, Washington Hall was filled and the two nights following found people almost hanging from the rafters. We had simply never heard anyone like him, never been so touched by stories so foreign but so able to engage both mind and heart.

The morning of the final lecture I was to meet him for breakfast at the Morris Inn where he was staying. I was excited but also nervous as breakfast time arrived. He is a thin, short man with salt and pepper hair and he holds your attention, but also gives you his. We talked about the book; he had already by then published more than a dozen books.

I told him my background, that I had studied Hebrew and the Hebrew Testament. He told me that he had been apprehensive about coming to Notre Dame. As a child he had crossed the street to be away from the Catholic church in Sighet. But his respect for Father Hesburgh, the response of the Notre Dame audience to his talks, and his good feeling about the book and the Press, had taken away any apprehensions he might have had.

For my part, I know this to be a fact. I have never met anyone as genuine and charismatic as this man. Subsequent years saw this initial meeting grow into a true and lasting friendship. Had he asked me then to go, sell everything I had, and come follow him, I think I would have done so.

In his book, *Four Hasidic Masters*, he describes the Holy Seer of Lublin in these words:

> ...he established no dynasty of his own. His disciples became leaders in their own right. People flocked to him from near and far, even from nonreligious circles...extremely perceptive and eloquent, he was unquestionably charismatic; he seemed always to be the center of his surroundings. His entire being radiated wisdom, beauty and authority. He rarely said "I" — rather, he said "We"...There was something regal about his personality. In his presence, one felt shaken, purified...transformed...

Were I a much better writer than I am, I could have written these exact words about Elie Wiesel.

—8—

Back in the Classroom

With the Press gaining prominence on campus and in the academic world, I was able to entertain an invitation to join the teaching faculty of the Core course in the College of Arts and Letters. I had already taught a course on publishing at the invitation of the amiable Don Costello, Chair of the American Studies Department. But this was an opportunity to teach two sections of Core and I could not resist. I scheduled the classes to meet at times when they would only minimally interfere with my work at the Press. And I made sure that the salary for my teaching would be paid to the Press and not to me. I was, after all, teaching on Press time.

The Core course was required of all sophomores in the College of Arts and Letters. It was a two-semester course that involved a lot of reading, discussion and writing of papers. The books selected for the syllabus were recognized classics in each field that the college offered as majors. So began a 20-year experience that was easily one of the highlights of my life. I suppose if I totaled it up, in my entire 20 years, I taught fewer than 800 students. It wasn't the numbers that mattered, it was that each section aimed at a maximum of 20 students so that the readings and discussions would allow students to get to know each other, to debate with accuracy, humility and civility, and to enjoy our excursion into matters of mind and spirit, matters about ideas that are part of our heritage, civilization, and moral development.

I told the class on the first day to take a look around the room. Believe it or not, I noted, these are the people you will most want to see when you come back to campus for class reunions. The class was challenging and lively. Students from some of the other sections complained that Core was boring. Our sections were never boring.

As I look back, my students included some of the most amazing people I ever knew. I learned from them and their life experiences as they supplied perspectives on issues worth caring about. I have stayed in touch with some of them and seen how they brought their values with them as they went on with their life. I think there is something special about Notre Dame students, something I didn't detect at St. Thomas College or the University of Michigan. I don't know how to describe it; I know that it is, but not exactly what it is. Were I to go back in time and list them, this would read like a phone book. I will settle for recalling faces and spirits that almost always brought me joy.

I think teaching is a sacred profession and it grieves me to see qualified people underserving their students at whatever the level, from grade school to graduate school. I think teachers have to reach beyond the techniques and technics that can provide facts and avenues to rudimentary knowledge. I think the teacher has to bring out wisdom and respect for the search that can lead to truth.

I always had good communication with my students; I wanted to know them and to model an excitement for ideas. I wanted them to decide what they will stand for in their life—and what they won't stand for.

At Notre Dame, the students do teacher-course evaluations at the end of every semester. I found their comments and suggestions encouraging and helpful. I was not an easy grader, especially on the papers they had to write. But neither was I there to help fight against grade inflation. I was there to teach. And to learn.

I always received high marks on the teacher evaluations. In the year 2000, my class evaluated me with a 4 point, or perfect, score. The committee in charge of the Arts and Letters Kaneb teaching awards sent one of their members to observe my class. Apparently he was impressed and I was named a Kaneb Award winner. I am not above including here the letter announcing that award. I treasure it because it reminds me of the students I taught. I ended every semester's last class by telling them: "I love you and I will be here rooting for you as long as I live." I meant it.

OFFICE OF THE PROVOST
UNIVERSITY OF NOTRE DAME
NOTRE DAME, INDIANA 46556-0399

April 25, 2000

Dr. James Langford
21550 New Road
Lakeville, IN 46536

Dear James:

On behalf of the University community, let me congratulate you on being selected as a 2000 Kaneb Award winner for your signal contribution to excellence in undergraduate education at the University of Notre Dame. You join an exceptionally talented cohort of educators across the University and we are deeply indebted to you for your energy and commitment to our teaching mission. As you know, the award carries with it a prize of $1,000.00, which will be distributed to you in the form of either a check or a direct deposit to your bank account. A recent review of the IRS tax code indicates that this is a taxable award.

Once again, I wish to extend my sincerest gratitude to you for your wonderful commitment to our common educational enterprise. Your effort rests at the heart of Notre Dame's mission in service to prepare outstanding leaders for our Church and our world.

Sincerely yours,

Rev. Timothy R. Scully, C.S.C.
Vice President and Senior Associate Provost

cc: Rev. Edward A. Malloy, C.S.C.
Nathan O. Hatch
Chris Fox
Steve Fredman

REV. TIMOTHY R. SCULLY, C.S.C. • VICE PRESIDENT AND SENIOR ASSOCIATE PROVOST
PHONE: 219-631-9002 • FAX: 219-631-6897 • E-MAIL: Scully.1@nd.edu

One of the philosophical bases of my approach to teaching was based on the triad I found in the writings of St. Thomas Aquinas. He divided the idea of "good" into three kinds of goods:

> *Bonum honestum* is the highest kind of good. It is good in itself...something like knowledge or love for its own sake.
>
> *Bonum delectabile* is good as enjoyed; pleasure, delight, gladness.
>
> *Bonum utile* is practical good; good that is readily useable, good that applies knowledge much as technology applies science.

I wanted what we learned in our readings and discussions to be good that touched all three kinds: to be worth having for its own sake, to be enjoyable and to be useful. It took a while into the first semester to develop this schema and the goal never was to reach an absolute consensus that confined thought to one mode or expression.

We were there not to memorize dogmas but to develop our own perspectives and to test them against the touchstones of civil and logical argumentation.

When I was a freshman at Notre Dame, all students in the College of Arts and Letters were required to take a course in Logic. Sadly, that is no longer the case; it is one requirement that never should have been dropped. How can one even read an article in the *New York Times* or hear a position voiced on Fox News without having quick recourse to seeing whether the premises truly lead to the conclusion drawn from them?

The world today has accelerated in scientific knowledge and the resulting technology. We can turn on a computer and see what is happening in far away parts of the world. We each have our own mobile phone and we can download all kinds of information and talk to anyone we dial. But what do we say? How do we verbalize and share what really matters to us? Teilhard de Chardin argued that, in some inextricable way, the world is being downsized, brought together, inexorably interrelated as never before. What happens to the Greek economy affects every economy in the world. Students today may see knowledge as useful, maybe enjoyable in some way, but less often than in the past as good for its own sake.

If we accept the testimony of the media, corruption has come to dominate politics, banks, law enforcement and courts. If the world is so out of control, does it mean that, left to ourselves, our penchant for evil will prevail? Is this the world the pseudo-Darwinists pictured—survival of the fittest—even if survival involves leaving the wounded, the needy, the aged and the poor behind? Do we need to protect ourselves from them? Such a dark picture! Not even random acts of kindness by those who have resources can color it or redeem it. When a society abandons the principles that once nurtured it, turns away from literature and the music of the ages, when we can no longer write a sentence without spellcheck or add without a machine, civility itself becomes a casualty.

These are issues that belong in the classroom. I submit that the gradual erosion of funding and respect for the humanities bodes poorly for our future. I have wrestled with these issues for decades. And here is my report:

Barely beneath the surface, in every land, I'll bet, in our country for sure, there is an army, a multitude of unsung, unknown, people of every race and class, every level of education, who strive to do their best every day, who care for the common good by caring for those who need help. These people are regular, not random, in their acts of kindness, in their commitment to make someone else's life better. These are people who know that real happiness is the smile on the face of someone surprised by your care.

I believe that human nature is basically good. Battered, but good. Maybe it just needs to be awakened, exercised and stretched. Maybe there is good news that needs to be spread. And maybe the young generations will be the ones who spread it.

To me, that is why the teaching profession is sacred.

Sometimes, if you let it happen, the students can turn the tables on you and help move your life to a place where eventually you discover the confluence of all three goods: worthy, enjoyable and practical. Let me give some background.

In 1979, my marriage fell apart; it had been fragile for several years. It became apparent that each of us had fallen in love with an ideal more than a person. When it became clear to each of us that our feet were clay, a mutual dislike set in. I made more mistakes than not and soon our differences were irreconcilable. I would not miss her, but I would very much miss Jeremy and Josh. My time with them was limited to every other weekend. A friend kept an eye on the neighborhood and alerted me when she spotted the boys riding their bikes so that I could sometimes get there to have a covert visit with them.

Eventually the marriage was annulled. As Timothy Schilling has written, "God our maker is also the God of our undoing. God has the clay in His hands. He can reshape it according to His will—or shatter the fired pot and start anew."

I moved to a friend's basement and then to an apartment near campus. My life was turned upside down. Again. I knew that I needed something to distract me from the pain I felt as I missed my sons.

Somewhere in the confines of my mind the idea came to me to combine my lifelong love of the Chicago Cubs with my talents as a writer of history. I checked the Archives of the Notre Dame Library and found that they had microfilm of the *Sporting News*, the *Chicago Tribune* and the *Sun-Times* and the *New York Times*—everything I would need for my research. And so began what would come to be *The Game Is Never Over: An Appreciative History of the Chicago Cubs, 1948-1980*.

Every day after my work at the Press, I headed to the microfilm room in the Library basement. I worked steadily until 12:00 when the Library closed. I took extensive notes by hand as I had done while researching for my Galileo book years before.

The players' names, trades, hopefuls and disappointments all came back to me and brought with them memories of my after-school race to get home in time to hear the last two or three innings of the game as described by Bert Wilson on station WIND, Chicago. Bert's mantra became mine: "The Game Is Never Over Until the Last Man Is Out." Because of all those days of listening and reading "The Cubs News," I remembered the players and could do more than cite averages; I could talk about them.

I opened the book with a Memo to Jeremy and Josh. It may seem corny now, but it says a lot about how much I love them and baseball.

Dear Sons:

It pleases me very much that you like baseball. Let me tell you why. Baseball has a lot of parallels to life. Watch it closely and you will learn a great deal about things like courage, beauty, strength, finesse, chance, fallibility and loyalty. Even at your young ages, you've rallied in the late innings and turned defeat into victory. You also know what it is like to lose suddenly, with one mistake, what had taken time and energy to build. You have schoolmates whose heart lifts them above their ordinary talents. And you know others who could do a lot better than they're doing but who don't seem to care. There are baseball players of both types; the ones fans admire are those who give all they have all the time.

You will see rookies whose agility allows them to challenge established players for a regular spot in the lineup. But note how cagey veterans use experience and know-how to fend off such a challenge, at least for another year. It is right that the young turks attempt to take over for their elders, but strength alone cannot displace wisdom.

Let your imagination run free. Fantasize yourself into games. Be the left fielder who makes a spectacular leaping catch at the wall to save the game...but sometimes imagine yourself as the hitter who gave it all he had only to be denied by that catch. You will have days in your life when you make two errors on the same play; remember, there is always a chance for redemption. I've seen players change boos to cheers with one swing of the bat. In baseball as in life there are advances and setbacks. Even in the midst of a losing streak there is assurance that, if we keep working at it, someday soon there will be cause for celebration. And winning streaks too must end.

It is good to learn that even the best-laid plans can run afoul of chance and circumstance. You will see easy grounders elude fielders by hitting a pebble in the infield; you'll watch home runs blown foul by a sudden gust of wind, and you will see games won or lost because of a checked-swing hit or the mistaken call of an umpire. There are things in life like that too. The best we can do is to rebound from them with grace.

Courage, anger, exhaustion and exuberance are part of every game, as they are of every life. If you study the records you will find that individual stars may dominate a team, but team play as a whole is the crucial factor in the final standings. No team has ever won a pennant without good utility players.

Be gentle in your judgment of our players; our protest must be directed not against them, but against the management, which either thinks that these guys are good or that we won't care if they're not.

At your age, Jeremy, I became addicted to baseball and the Cubs. I would race home from school so I could listen to the last innings of the game. As soon as the radio warmed up, there would be Bert Wilson describing the scene and I could tell by the tone of his voice whether we were ahead or behind. For my eleventh birthday, my dad gave me *The Complete Encyclopedia of Baseball*, a book I still treasure despite its vintage. There I studied and learned the past glories of the Cubs, though they now floundered at the bottom of the League. I have never wavered in my devotion to the Cubs. The game is never over until the last man is out.

The game has never been over for me. The game goes on through the winter until it takes up again at where it left off the previous season. Baseball is a celebration of hope. Maybe that's why the season begins in the spring.

The story of the Cubs in those years was largely one of endless hopes and failures. Owner Phil Wrigley didn't particularly like baseball. But he was good at selling gum.

There were some bright lights in the late 1960s, especially 1969, when the Cubs fielded a team that included names like Santo, Williams, Banks, Jenkins, Kessinger, Hundley, Holtzman, Hands and Hickman. Those were the days, at least until September 5 when they had a five-game lead over the New York Mets only to lose it and first place to the hated Mets on September 10. Four Cubs from that team made it to the Baseball Hall of Fame, but none of them made it to the World Series as a Cub.

I wrote in a way that blended history with a fan's viewpoint. Of course, there was some humor. When

Phil Wrigley, owner of the Cubs, learned that the book would be published, he had his representative, Salty Saltwell, inform me that I'd better be careful what I wrote about him. The reader likely knows how I feel about censorship. Still, my account of those Cub years was both accurate and warm even though it was not a whitewash.

Since no one else was bothering to write a history of those years in Cubs annals, the coast was clear. My book attracted widespread interest and sales. It made the Chicago best-seller list four times. Reviews, even from Chicago sportswriters, were all positive. They used words like "excellent," "accurate," " enjoyable," "a treasure," "a joy," and from Gene Shalit on *The Today Show*, "A love note to the Cubs...I loved it."

My favorite review was from Herb Michelson in the *Sacramento Bee*. He described the book as "caviar for the masochist" and "painful nostalgia."

And he concluded: "It is likely that only a Cub fan will care about this book. But that is okay. There are millions of us—not to mention thousands of other 'losers' who will revel in the empathy. Jim Langford has done a noble service to ineptitude. Bless him."

Sales were brisk and Icarus Press, owned by my friend Bruce Fingerhut, urged me to add an update for the paperback edition which came out in 1982. The publicity manager for Icarus was Jill Justice and she and I fell in love.

By the time the paperback appeared, the fans' chant "Double your pleasure, double your fun, sell the Cubs in '81" had come true. Wrigley sold the franchise to the *Chicago Tribune*. The new owners turned to Dallas Green to leave the Philadelphia Phillies and become General Manager of the Cubs. He vowed to start a new tradition—a winning tradition. And he did. His trades were bountiful; it became clear that the Cubs were on a different track now. I finished my update for the paperback by writing: "I'll bet Ransom Jackson's autograph that the Cubs will win it all in 1984. We are ready. Go Cubs."

Two years later, it was 1984 and the Cubs made me seem to be a baseball prophet. These Cubs, Dallas Green's Cubs, performed beyond optimistic expectations. They had quality players and great spirit. In the playoffs, all they had to do was to beat the San Diego Padres in a best-of-five game series. The winner would face the Detroit Tigers in the World Series. The first two games were at Wrigley Field and the Cubs won both of them. Jill and I were there to see Game Two of the playoffs. We needed to win one of the three games to be played in San Diego to be National League Champions for the first time since 1945.

—9—

Oprah, Diamond and a Camp

As word spread in the media that I had predicted the Cubs success two years in advance, my status as a Cubs historian and prophet was confirmed. I started fielding numerous calls asking for phone interviews on radio sports talk shows across the country. But there was one call in particular that, in hindsight, was the best of them.

I received a call from the producer of a TV talk show in Chicago asking me to be on the show on Monday morning to lead the celebration of the Cubs winning the pennant. The fifth and deciding game was to be played on Sunday. I asked again, "What show is it?" She repeated, "The Oprah Show." This was before Oprah went national. I asked, "Who else will be on the show?" She said, "Stars from the cast of *All My Children.*"

I had seen segments of that soap opera and liked the cast. I said, "OK, Yes."

They put us up at the Knickerbocker Hotel on Sunday and we watched the game there. The Cubs were winning into the eighth inning behind our star pitcher Rick Sutcliffe. It was easy to see that he was getting tired. Steve Trout, who had been masterful in beating the Padres in Game Two at Wrigley, was warmed up in the bullpen and ready to come into the game. But Manager Jim Frey stuck with the weary Sutcliffe on the theory that, as he said later, "You dance with the one who brung ya." The sad ending is that the Padres rallied and won. Heartbroken, I called the producer and asked whether she still wanted me on the show. She said, "Absolutely. We booked you and you need to be here." Instead of leading a celebration, our mission would be to console. In the morning a limo picked us up and took us to the Harpo Studio. I tried to think of words to say that would ease the pain of the crushing Cubs loss.

One image or myth came to mind. It was the ancient myth of Sisyphus who had insulted the gods and was sentenced to spend time and eternity rolling a huge boulder up a mountainside in an attempt to reach the top.

Each time he got close, the gods would make sure the boulder would slip away and fall to the bottom. Sisyphus would have to go back down and start all over. Repeatedly. Forever. But he was superior to his fate. Instead of being downtrodden, he smiled and renewed his task. It seemed to me to be the perfect metaphor for Cubs fans on this morning after. The studio audience received it with appreciation. As for Oprah, she was charming, welcoming and warm. I thoroughly enjoyed the experience.

My book *The Game Is Never Over*, The Cub Fan's Calendar, the Oprah Show and some pieces I wrote for the Cubs Program Magazine earned us an invitation to the Cubs annual Old-Timers party at the downtown Hilton. It was a preview of Eden. There we were mixing with my heroes from decades of devotion. I brought a copy of my book and asked for autographs. The signers include Jack Brickhouse, Ernie Banks, Ron Santo, Don Kessinger, Billy Williams, Hank Sauer, Moose Moryn, Bill Hands, Milt Pappas, Andy Pafko, José Cardenal, Peanuts Lowrey and Bob Will. Obviously I treasure that book and the whole 1984 experience. Perhaps even George Orwell would agree, it was a great year.

In 1982, Jill and I had founded a book publishing company which we named Diamond Communications. Jill was the sole owner and president. I notified the General Counsel at Notre Dame and, since the University Press does not publish sports books, Mr. Phil Faccenda wrote back that there was no conflict of interest.

One of the first publications was my creative venture The Cub Fan's Calendar: A Nostalgic, Humorous and Loving Guide to the Year—for Cub Fans Only. All the research I had done for *The Game Is Never Over and The Cub Fan's Guide to Life* now found a new outlet in this oversized, black-and-white calendar with monthly themes based in history and humor and salient quotes from past and present Cubs, and selected dates remembering trades, Cub heroics and bobbles, and celebrating the ever-optimistic nature of Cub fans. It was an immediate hit and it took off in Chicago thanks to Roy Leonard of WGN radio. Roy, one of the true gentlemen in the radio talk-show business, did a 30-minute in-studio interview with me on the day after Thanksgiving—a prime day for Christmas shopping. We had so much fun, he had me back the day after Thanksgiving every year for the next decade, each time finding delight in the calendar. Sales of the calendar were so good that Jill had the capital to begin publishing books, mostly about baseball, and Diamond quickly became a recognized and respected imprint.

We were careful to avoid use of the Cubs' trademarks and we stayed in touch with Jeff Odenwald, Director of Marketing in the Cubs front office. Jeff understood that the calendar was a good way to keep Cub fans in touch throughout the year.

As Diamond began to grow, the garage and basement became crowded with boxes of books. Chicago was a very good book market.

In addition to 16 Kroch's and Brentano's stores, there was Marshall Field's and numerous independent stores. Later Walden Books and B. Dalton appeared. Those were heady days for those publishing books on Chicago themes. Diamond gained prominence by publishing two books by beloved Detroit Tigers broadcaster Ernie Harwell, one by Jack Brickhouse and another by Chuck Thompson, the play-by-play man for the Baltimore Orioles for many years. This attention to baseball broadcasters attracted Curt Smith to publish with Diamond his classic work, *Voices of the Game,* a detailed and delightful history of baseball broadcasting. Diamond went on to publish books on Notre Dame football, women's basketball, and tennis. All of this made it necessary to look for property in the countryside, not far from South Bend, where Diamond could build a more suitable storage facility and where I could find peace and quiet to abet my own writing.

In 1992, we found the perfect property, an old farm with 16 acres, a quarter of a mile up a narrow lane. I put up a sign down at the end of the lane where it met New Road. It said simply "Private Property. If we don't know you are coming, turn around here."

This was a place with silence built into its ambiance. I told friends that the 12-mile drive to Notre Dame for work at the Press and in the classroom was nothing compared to the peace of being in the country.

Interestingly enough, one day when I was working on the grounds, a car came up the lane and four gentlemen dressed in suit and tie got out. I asked them whether they had read the sign at the end of the lane. The answer was "Yes, but it doesn't matter; Jesus sent us." To which I answered, "Well Jesus didn't tell me you were coming, so I have to ask you to leave." They did so. The moral of the story is that no matter how far away you move or how hidden your abode may be, Jehovah's Witnesses will find you.

All of the preceding account of moving to the country to find peace and quiet is just a way to introduce the story of how my students helped change my life.

One of the books on the syllabus in Core was *There Are No Children Here*, a Pulitzer Prize-winning account of children growing up in the projects of Chicago. The author, Alex Kotlowitz, recounts how the title came about. He was interviewing one of the mothers in the public housing which was built to accommodate indigent, almost exclusively black, people. Kotlowitz noticed that there were not many youngsters playing in the area and he asked where the children were. She responded to the effect that there were no children here because they aren't able to be children. They stay inside for protection from drugs, random gunshots and other forms of harm.

It is an accurate and passionate picture of what it is like to grow up in such a place. Children are too easily disposable; funeral insurance is bought as part of the food budget. It can't be that this is part of America, at least not the America my students knew. Most of them were from well-to-do families. Most of them had no idea of what it must be like to have to scratch to stay alive. Most of them were white.

The first time I read the book, I experienced

something no other book had ever done to me. I cried.

I was anxious to hear how the students would react to reading it.

Though I expected that some would be touched by it, I was happily surprised that their reaction was much deeper and all-inclusive than that. Their souls were burned by this book. Their initial reaction was one of amazement, almost to the point of incredulity. How could this be true? This is happening ninety miles from us. And then the really salient question, "What can we do about this?" The easy answer would have been to point out: "You are students at a great university; you will all be leaders in our society. You can work to come up with economic, social, and legal changes that will make this a bad dream." But something more was needed.

First of all, I pointed out, we don't have to go to Chicago to find the sadness of such poverty and its consequences. On a smaller scale, but equally awful, the same conditions, the same kinds of deprivation, the same circumstances crushing the hopes and happiness of children, exist right here in South Bend, or Elkhart, Benton Harbor, Michigan City and LaPorte, to name a few. So let's invest a couple more class periods trying to figure out what we can do to help.

When I got home I described the class discussion to Jill, who had read the book, and asked for her input so that I could hear her ideas. In the next two days, things began to become clear to me. I found the brief passage that had jumped off the page at me when I first read it. It describes how ten-year-old Pharaoh Rivers found a spot three blocks from the Horner Project where he lived, a spot where he could think and daydream and feel safe, if only for a while:

> Three blocks from Horner sits a condominium complex called Damen Courts. Its manicured lawns and graffiti-free walls seem immaculate next to the rubble of Horner...the grass carpet offered a quiet resting place; it was like going to the beach. Pharaoh found a shady place on the lawn and shot marbles or read a "Captain America" or "Superman" comic. Or, if the mood fit him, he just sat and daydreamed...
>
> He wanted a place that he could escape to by himself, where nothing would interrupt his daydreaming, where no one would try to fight him, where he didn't have to worry about gunshots or firebombings. (p.143)

I said to Jill, "We have acres of grass...all we need is to bring the children." I told my students that if they help, we will start a day camp and bring inner-city and disadvantaged children to be carefree for a day or an afternoon, to explore the woods without fear of molestation or bullies or gunshots or violence. We would help them play games for enjoyment and introduce them to college volunteers who care, who will listen, befriend and make the experience one with magic in it. The students loved the idea. But at that point it was still only an idea; much work needed to be done, networking had to begin, and some unexpected battles would have to be fought.

First we needed a name and a logo for the camp. In honor of Alex Kotlowitz's book, we decided to name it "There Are Children Here." The logo, designed by Juanita Dix, was pleasantly evocative.

Having just built a new house attached to the old house on the property, our money was in short supply. I did not know anything about how to raise money, except for my days at Holy Rosary where Bingo did the trick.

Then I remembered Tom Suddes, a former director in the Notre Dame Development Office, who had recently hired our son Josh for his company in Ohio, and who is an expert in fundraising for non-profit organizations. Tom invited me to attend a seminar he would be giving in Chicago. He taught so much in one day that it was somewhat daunting. But he kept repeating the question, "What is the worst thing that can happen if you ask someone or some organization for money?" The answer, of course, was nothing worse than a "No."

His last challenge to us was to ask for something we really needed and to make a good case for a yes answer.

I had been looking in the classified ads for a used tractor/mower. No sooner had I returned from Chicago than an ad appeared in the For Sale classifieds for a used Kubota tractor with a mowing deck and also a large blade on the front. At that time this machine brand new would sell for about $7,000. The used version listed in the ad was $1,700. I wanted it. I needed it. And we could not afford it. Remembering the Suddes mantra, I called the owner and asked if I could see it. He said, "Sure." I took with me the prospectus I had drawn up for the camp. The seller's name was Andy Karafa. He had taken excellent care of the Kubota, which was about six years old. He showed me how to operate it and let me test drive it around his ample acres. Before I began the drive I handed Mr. Karafa the camp prospectus and I explained that we had secured a preliminary approval from the IRS to register as a not-for-profit 501c3 organization. As I drove around I saw that he was reading the prospectus. So I kept driving.

Finally I steered back and confessed that I loved that machine and I not only wanted it, I needed it. I asked him whether I could make monthly payments as donations came in for the camp. He paused and said, "Let me think about it. Can you give me a reference at Notre Dame I can call and check you out?" I said without hesitation, "Father Ted Hesburgh, the President." I don't know whether he called Fr. Ted but he called me that evening and said that he would donate the Kubota to the camp. Then came a humorous wrinkle: After thanking him I said, "I don't have any way to get the tractor over to the camp site." He laughed and replied, "OK. I'll deliver it."

The process of incorporating TACH with the state in 1994, and seeking non-profit status from the IRS had intimidated me into seeking help from a friend, Dave Link, Dean of the Law School at Notre Dame. Dean Link's name on the application would carry weight just as a CPA does on a tax return. We were accepted.

The *South Bend Tribune* printed a small story about the plan for the camp and apparently it set off a person who lived across New Road who didn't want inner-city kids coming to her part of the country. She never talked to me in person or by phone. Instead she concentrated on trying to rally people against us.

She had called the County Zoning Commission and they said that our property was not zoned for use as a camp. The commissioner called me and I went to his office to file the forms for a rezoning permit. A hearing before the Area Plan Commission was scheduled. They were charged with recommending for or against rezoning request and providing that to the County Council.

Unaware that there would be any opposition, I went to the Area Plan hearing by myself. We did not expect any problem. I was surprised to see people I recognized from the New Road area. They came prepared, armed with a petition drawn up by the woman across the road. She had gone house to house, farm to farm, warning that we would be bringing work-release prisoners (probably because our newsletter said that we would be working with Open Door, which is a preschool for children with special needs). They said that busloads of children from Chicago and Detroit would be coming and obviously they would soon be marauding through nearby fields in search of trouble.

She and her cohorts showed up at the Area Plan hearing. Five of them were remonstrators who argued against the rezoning. I had to listen to them say that, while they thought our intentions were "commend-able," they were worried about "the safety of the children." One went so far as to say that there were "sinkholes" on our property that would swallow up the children; another said the presence of children would scare away the wildlife and she might not be able to look out the window and see deer coming off our property. She also pointed out that since there already was a summer camp for handicapped children 15 miles away, there was no need for "another one."

In private they admitted to some people who refused to join them, that they didn't want black children in the area out of fear that maybe their older siblings would start coming out and the crime rate would go up. My presentation was straightforward. The camp seeks to aid the entire community. It is more than a quarter of a mile from the home of any of the opponents, and, if there was a sinkhole why had that individual let his children play in there when they were youngsters?

The Area Plan Commission decided not to decide. They sent it on to the County Council for a hearing and a decision.

I went home thoroughly disappointed. I told Jill that we should put our place up for sale and move somewhere that wasn't peopled with bigots. Neither of us wanted to move. We decided that it was important that we stay and fight the exaggerations, untruths, fears and the real motivation behind the opposition. I cannot characterize my mood that night as happy.

Then something quite remarkable happened. The

next evening there was a knock at the door. I opened it to see our neighbor to the north of us, Elson Fish standing there. I invited him in and he told me that he and his wife had prayed about the issue and concluded that the Lord would want this camp here. His faith had trumped their negativity. That is what faith really looks like in the real world.

Elson promised to stand with us at the County Council hearing and to contact the commissioner from our district. We started receiving calls and letters from people who live in the area and who wanted us to know that they supported us. Neighbors who own almost all the property that was anywhere near ours held meetings, invited the remonstrators, contacted the Council representative from our district, and let everyone know that they wanted this program "in their backyard."

The time arrived for a hearing at the County Council. This time I went to a hearing fully prepared. I had with me leaders of a number of community agencies who testified that this camp was sorely needed. Dean Link was there and spoke briefly. Thirty or forty Notre Dame students were there to lend support. The Council was impressed; the hearing turned into a love-in. We left with a unanimous decision in favor of rezoning.

In the 17 years the camp hosted children, not one child or volunteer or guest even set foot outside the camp property. Traffic was never an issue and neither was noise, assuming one would describe children's glee from a quarter of a mile away as "noise." No sinkholes either.

It was a lesson well learned: do not let negativity, however disguised, stop you from doing what you know is right. And another lesson: believe in people and their goodness by remembering those who came forth at the darkest moment to offer help. I cannot begin to say how much that support and its timing meant to us.

With that nonsense out of the way, we could now turn our attention to designing the camp and raising the money to build it. The Kubota proved its worth on day one and every day for 17 years.

The blade helped remove debris as we built bike paths through the nine acres of woods. The mower kept the grass mowed just right for play, and the older kids loved driving it—if only for a few yards.

Andy Karafa, if you didn't know it before, you do now. The echoes of thousands of kids having fun are a chorus of thanks to you.

We spent the next year preparing the facilities without impeding the comings and goings of our young guests. If this was to be their country club, it had better be first class. We discovered that if it costs too much to have professional excavators clear the playing fields and clean up the woods, have chain-saw parties, get volunteers, and do it yourself. Offers of goods and services as well as support began to pour in. The zeal of those who came to help rekindled and enriched our own faith. The place itself seemed especially blessed.

I had to learn quickly how to write successful grant applications.

It took a year before we raised the money to build a

clubhouse, complete with lavatories, a kitchen, a fire-place and a porch. Goodness abounded: the kitchen cabinets, carpet, plumbing, and insulation were do-nated by various suppliers. It came together quickly and ended up costing $42,000. Local TV stations came out and covered the opening of the clubhouse. Word was getting around that TACH was filling a glaring gap in local services for at-risk children. We began long- term relationships with the Boys and Girls Club of St. Joseph County and their after-school sites at el-ementary schools including Harrison, Perley, Wilson, and Battell, as well as the main site on E. Sample St. We also hosted Head Start from the Hansel Center, the Center for the Homeless, Grace Community Center, La Casa de Amistad, and LaVille elementary. Each group of kids came with a staff member from their agency so we had someone who knew them and their needs, allergies and so forth. Before long, we connected with grade schools in the project areas of Chicago through the Inner City Teaching Corps. They brought kids and their teachers to spend whole weekends at TACH.

I remember breaking into tears when the first group of kids ever to come to TACH were leaving on the school bus and their little hands were waving goodbye and their faces were alive with smiles. My tears were of joy and sadness. I had seen them here and I knew what many of them were going back to. I don't know if I ever got over that contrast.

Many of the students in my Core Course made TACH their own. And perhaps not by chance alone, it was the men of often-maligned Zahm Hall who led the way. Zahm was known for characters and sometimes zany antics. I knew the men of Zahm to be of strong character and sometimes zany antics. It was Tony McCanta who led the zahmbies to TACH. We flew the Zahm Hall flag on our flagpole.

Zahm men voted to donate money from pizza sales and fundraisers to TACH. Volunteer leaders emerged, first Tony McCanta, then Paul Nebosky; they were aided by Vern Walker, Bill Hennessy, J.P. Jarczyk, Jon Donnelly, Chris Costigan, the Amato brothers, Joe Saenz, Andrew Sherman, Mike Smith, Chris Walker and Wally Poirer, who wrote shortly before his untimely death as a Peace Corps volunteer in Bolivia, "I wish I had spent more time at TACH. I left there feeling better than any other place I have ever passed a second."

Varsity athletes often came to help. Troy Murphy, Jimmy Friday, Darrell Campbell, Jeff Faine, and Brennan Curtin were among them. I remember one occasion when the kids were acting up in the clubhouse. I told them that they'd better stop because my bodyguard was coming. They laughed at me. Then Brennan Curtin, all 6'8", 285 pounds of him, came walking in the door. They were impressed. Silence reigned until one kid pointed out the obvious: "Wow. You're big!"

And the women volunteers from Notre Dame were just as generous with their time and their hearts. Paola Ramirez, Liz Halligan, Rachel Bundick, Kim Sides, Katie Fuehrmeyer, Sharon Watson, Silvy Un, and the Moschel sisters, Michelle and Marissa, were some of many. So were Beth Farthing, Anne Hosinski and Shannon Marks. I watched over a period of two years how the Moschels turned a shy boy with low self-esteem who came from the Grace Center into a popular, confident and amiable young man. I don't know if they realize how much they changed the course of his life.

Of course I cannot list all of the volunteers who joined us. By my calculations, there were about 1000 volunteer stints at the camp every year.

On many of the fund-raising grant applications there are requests to quantify the results of your organization's efforts. For us, the results were real but not countable. I usually responded to those requests by noting the quotient we count is the smiles and sounds that light up the camp every day. By those standards, we top the charts. Patricia Kelly Holmes helped us raise money.

It was good for our Trevor and Emily too. They were there on a daily basis and made friends that remember them fondly many years later.

As for me, TACH became the highlight of my days, even more than publishing or teaching. I loved all three things that I did: publishing, teaching and the camp, and I gave myself to each of them as fully as I could. I did not realize at the time that there were tolls to pay. I was 57 years old when the camp started in 1994, and though each part of my life energized me, at the end of the day I was tired. When I am tired I am cranky. In a way, I neglected my family, Jill and all four children. I don't think that is an argument for celibacy as much as it is for more and better awareness and common sense.

If the children from the South Bend area loved coming to "the farm" as they called it, for the children who came from the neighborhoods in Chicago, thanks to the Inner-City Teaching Corps whose teachers came with their students, the effect of the camp was magic. They brought sleeping bags and slept on the floor of the clubhouse. For many of them, the ones from the Projects, it was the first time they had really seen the stars in the sky. The lights of the city blocked that view; the open spaces of the country let them see the sky full of shining stars.

There were miracles for certain, some major, some minor, each stunning in its own way. When it was time to build a little-league baseball field, I wrote Joan Kroc of McDonald's, whose late husband was an ardent baseball fan and, for a time, owner of the San Diego Padres. I told her about the camp and our field and that we needed funds to do it right. She sent a check that covered building the field and buying equipment!

The children and the college students enjoyed playing baseball, but they made it clear that what they really wanted to play was basketball. It was equally clear that we did not have sufficient funds to build an asphalt basketball court. I said that, if necessary, we'll have to seek a loan. I started the process of getting cost estimates from asphalt companies and quality backboard suppliers. The bids were not encouraging.

Then something unbelievable happened. On the

very day that an envelope containing the winning bid was in our mailbox, the envelope immediately underneath it brought us a check for $5,000 from an anonymous donor, through the St. Joseph County Community Foundation. The total cost of building the court was $5,050.

Next came the donation by UPS, of two magnificent metal bleachers, one for the baseball field, one for the basketball court. We brought in 20 tons of sand and built a volleyball court (when the younger kids were there, they used it as a giant sandbox).

I could fill a book with wonderful stories and sad stories emanating from the camp and its people. There is no sweeter noise than the children talking to each other in the sandbox, kidding each other on the basketball court, or the squeals of children being pulled through the woods in a big farm wagon. And there is no sadder sound than hearing a child recite the violence and horrors they have seen or experienced. As Jonathan Kozol has written, children "do not die as easily as we might have believed. No matter what we do to cheat and injure them, they light their little lights and...tell us that the beautiful illumination of their souls is not so readily eclipsed as we may think."

Their stories are often very complex. The majority are from families that have experienced violence, drugs, poverty and hopelessness. Two of the children who were regulars at the camp were murdered, two others had lost their mothers to murder. The dropout rate in the schools they attend is 48%. As Mother Teresa pointed out, "We think sometimes that poverty is only being hungry, naked and homeless. The poverty of being unwanted, unloved and uncared for is the greatest poverty." These children carry more baggage at the age of ten than most people accrue in a lifetime. Some are in their third or fourth foster home, others are being raised by grandmothers because their parents are dead, in prison or living far away.

But they come with resources too. They are survivors; their instincts can detect genuine care and, though slowly, they respond to it deeply and with gratitude. Most look out for each other, always looking for fairness in how they and others are treated. Nearly all display a sense of humor that helps rescue them from sadness or terror. I remember one occasion when several black kids were in the crow's nest above the swing and slide set. One of the white kids began to climb up the slide to the nest only to be told that "no whites are permitted up here." I went over and started climbing the slide so I could talk to them only to hear the race monitor say, "It's OK. Jim's not white."

Let me illustrate what I am saying by telling a story:

Markus is a ten-year-old who was at TACH on a weekend for kids from the Projects in Chicago. His body language, the way he walks, tells you he is old for his age. He sizes things up quickly; his eyes take in the situation and he is always alert, even edgy. He is from the other Chicago, the one that lives behind the face of tall buildings where, sixty years ago, blacks were moved into what was an urban equivalent of Indian reservations. Over time they became hellholes of death, despair and destitution. As usual, the victims were blamed for their plight.

It doesn't take long to realize that Markus is destined to be a leader. He is strong, determined, confident and blessed with a sense of humor that he uses to shield himself in moments of sadness or discomfort in new surroundings. The other nine children in the group look up to him—a few with apprehension because he is volatile, most with admiration because he is forceful. Markus is one of the children we absolutely have to reach; he will play a key role in the ongoing battle between good and evil. But listen to what happened to him in a 12-month span surrounding his visit to the camp.

The project buildings were being demolished and the tenants are being moved to smaller, more dispersed public housing. Markus's building is one of the first to go and so he and his family moved out of the only home they had known. Of course it was a move up, but it also meant taking new bearings and discovering the street rules for the new, nearly as-dangerous neighborhood.

During the school year, his teachers were determined to find out why he did so poorly in school. They convinced his mother to let him be tested. It was discovered that he is dyslexic. Just as more tests were scheduled, the principal came to his classroom, took him to the office and told him he needed to go home. It was his aunt. She had just been murdered, thrown out of a forth-floor window by her boyfriend.

Markus doesn't grieve; he says he's fine and shows smiles to prove it.

The testing stops, but the teachers continue to breach the walls and salve his aches before they become calluses. Finally, he cries.

As the school year winds down, word comes that his school, a Catholic grade school in the inner city, is to be closed for financial reasons. One more hitching post for hope is pulled up and Markus is set adrift again.

What will happen to him now? Will other teachers care for him as these did? Two sides are already wrestling for his spirit—one reveals good manners, obvious care for his friends whom he shields and protects; the other shows a quick willingness to use force to claim his place.

There he is, with his slightly cocky demeanor, his pick-comb lodged beneath his baseball cap, his eyes flashing, ready to smile—or to strike.

In June of 1997, when the camp was three years old, Steve Kloehn, Religion writer for the *Chicago Tribune*, penned a front-page story in the Tempo section about my new book, *Happy Are They: Living the Beatitudes in America*. The story focused on the account of TACH in that book. Alex Kotlowitz, who lives in Oak Park, read the piece and wrote me a kind and complimentary letter. He said: "I've often told my life that someday I'd like to live in the country where I could write and work with kids. You are living that dream." We stayed in touch over time, especially when he accepted an invitation to teach a course at Notre Dame. He is a remarkable man and I am grateful to have met him.

One year after the *Chicago Tribune* piece appeared, thanks to a connection initiated by my son Jeremy, Judy Valente, the Midwest reporter for the PBS TV show *Religion and Ethics NewsWeekly*, hosted by Bob Abernathy, asked to do a segment about the camp. It turned out to be a wonderful telling of our story which Judy and her crew conducted perfectly.

I'm not certain which exposure, the *Chicago Tribune*, a feature in *Notre Dame Magazine*, or PBS, caught the attention of a scout for George Bush's campaign in 2000, but one day I received a call from a gentleman asking whether he could come and observe the camp. I agreed. At that time, Mr. Bush was pushing the idea of starting an office in Washington which would serve as a liaison between the White House and religious non-profit organizations working on social issues. I could see that our visitor was quite impressed. Then came the moment of truth. He said that they were confident that Bush would win the election and they were looking around for the right person to direct the new office. He added that they were "looking for a compassionate conservative." All I could say in response was "Well, I am compassionate, but I'm not conservative." We parted amicably.

Although I retired from the University Press in 1999, I was asked to stay on for a year while the new director cleared up matters prior to her move from Columbus, Ohio. I agreed. I continued to teach, and when I turned the Press over to the incoming director, I accepted an offer from Psychology Professor George Howard to join him in a research position which lasted for two more years. Of course I missed the Press and the good people who were my colleagues in that work: Jeff Gainey, John Ehmann, Ann Rice, Diane Schaut, Greg Rockwell, Marge Gloster, Ann Bromley, Betty

Scates, Carol Roos, Donald Doland, Kathy Jun, Paula Billet and Gina Bixler.

In the meantime, I had an idea driven by my conviction that there are a multitude of people out there doing positive things trying to build a better world. I wanted to meet some of them, mostly from our area, and tell their stories in a book. I formed it around the Beatitudes from the Sermon on the Mount. It worked out that each profile focused on a person who had explicitly set out to make a difference. I wanted to introduce and proclaim the other side, the good side of the news.

My son, Jeremy, pitched in. We interviewed a dozen people who had stepped forward to help others in special ways. One man started a "free" store for people in need of clothes and basics. He collected, cleaned and gave away goods in a storefront a friend had loaned him. Another was founder and director of a home to train and nurture unwed mothers; still another founded a center to reduce violence between teens. An older gentleman set out to buy and rehab homes for the homeless, and a man in Minneapolis who organized the needy, taught them about jobs, savings, paying bills, and living responsibly. And there was a doctor who returned from the University of Chicago Medical School to his small town community. He started a community medical clinic, gave ownership to the people, took a modest salary, and provided excellent and inexpensive care.

I will admit that, as I began the book project, I was hoping to profile a few non-religious humanists. But I did not find any. Every one of our interviewees was motivated by his or her religious beliefs.

Although the book garnered strong reviews, it never caught on with the public. Sad to say, the print, social and television media all focus on the Kardashians and Duggars and not on the real lives most all of us live.

—10—

A Fragile World

Early in the new school year came the disaster of 9/11/2001. Like everyone else, I was dumbfounded. It was hard to know what to do. I elected to go to the Grotto at Notre Dame and join the throng of students, faculty and staff who were gathering there. This must have been somewhat like what Americans felt on December 7, 1941, when Pearl Harbor was attacked. Every day there were new stories of sorrow and heroism. Every day the heavens were bombarded with questions beginning with the main one: Why?

I wanted to listen to the leading theological thinkers of our time to see how they reacted to this horror. What might wise believers say about it?

By the end of the year I contacted my good friend Leroy Rouner at Boston University and suggested we put together a book under the title *Walking with God in a Fragile World*. We asked world-renowned believers to write original essays for the book. The response was inspiring. We were able to publish original reflections of Elie Wiesel, Father Theodore Hesburgh, Karen Armstrong, Wendy Doniger, Frederick Buechner, William Sloane Coffin, Stanley Hauerwas, Father Virgil Elizondo and Jürgen Moltmann, among others. I worked with Father Hesburgh on his essay and received this letter which I cherish:

Jim Langford
Consulting Editor
Religious Studies/Philosophy
21550 New Road
Lakeville, Indiana 46536

Dear Jim:

Your are a worthy son of your father, Walter, and your mother, Dit.

I thought you caught the spirit of what we discussed perfectly. I only have a few very minor corrections to make.

Many thanks for your wonderful generosity in doing this. I totally endorse what you have written but I think you make me a little better than I am.

Many thanks, again,

Ever devotedly in Notre Dame,

Father Ted

(Rev.) Theodore M. Hesburgh, C.S.C.
President Emeritus

When it came out in 2003, it did not sell widely, but it deeply touched those who read it.

Although I was healing faster than expected from recent heart surgery, I had trouble being happy. In fact, I was downright mean. I don't know why that was, or whether it is a common response among survivors of that surgery, but I know I was not easy to live with at that point. Part of it was, for me, spiritual. It seemed to me that I had been hiding from the very God I was trying to serve, the God I had known years before. It was as though tinted scales had grown over my eyes and I no longer cared to or could see clearly with the eyes of faith. Still, I never really stopped believing, never denied the grace I sensed was operative in my life, especially at the camp. The signs were there every day, occasionally with undeniable clarity. Once, when we had nearly exhausted the supply of food at the camp, a station wagon pulled up to the clubhouse and two women I had never seen before unloaded boxes and boxes of food. They drove away before I could reach them and thank them. To this day I think they were angels; they certainly acted like angels and, as Aristotle had noted in ancient times, "As a thing acts, so it is."

My "crisis of faith" eventually passed and the tinted scales dissolved so I could again read what was happening with the open eyes of faith.

And my faith was strengthened by seeing the love the Notre Dame students shared with the children at our camp.

One of our regular volunteers was a 280-pound

defensive tackle on the Irish football team. (I'll call him DC). I had alerted him to the situation of one of the fifth graders at a local school where we visited regularly. I asked him to help the boy (who I will call Q) any way he could. A few months later, DC sent me this email:

Q is a really good kid. I have been working with him extra hard and giving him positive reinforcement because, honestly, the women who run the program there don't give the kids enough of that. Last Thursday I ended up getting Q some candy because the other kids made fun of him for not having money to do so. The ladies working there were not even going to sell me the candy if I was going to give it to Q. They were adamant. I ended up lying to the teachers there, took Q to the side, gave him the candy and told him not to tell anyone; he tucked it away in his pocket.

When I came back Monday, Q ran clear across the playground to give me a hug. He always asks about you, Professor Langford. He says, "Where's Jim? If he doesn't come with you next time tell him he's going to get a Pow from me," and he makes a fist and shakes it in my face. The teachers here label him as a trouble-maker and treat him as such. When I ask them "Has he been bad?" they reply "No, but he will be."

I've been hanging around with him and he tells me everything that is going on in his life. You know what he did with that piece of candy? He went home and broke it into pieces so he could share it with his brother. It was a treat his mother could not afford to give them. He tells me how life is not fun for him at home and how his mom met this guy who doesn't treat him, his siblings or his mom well. I love this little guy; my heart goes out to him every time I see him. The teachers have discarded him and constantly put him in timeout. They single him out with negative re-inforcement. The only way he knows how to respond to everybody being so mean to him is by fighting and giving people a POW so to speak.

He sees this at home, goes to school and gets it from teachers and classmates who learn from the ex-ample of the teachers. He is a really good kid. We are the only people who care about him and respond to him in a positive way. We don't judge, we don't single out, we just try to be good people and role models. We teach them by correcting behavior, we tell them to apologize, instruct them on why what they did was wrong and show them a better course of action. I re-ally feel for the kids going to this school.

Enough said.

When the teachers tried to prevent Q from being in the group coming to camp, I told them not to come unless Q was with them. He never misbehaved, ever, at the camp. No need to wonder why. All we can do now, ten years later, is to pray and hope for Q. We re-member him in his happy moments. We brought him joy...and he more than returned the favor.

Maybe it was bound to happen, maybe not, but in 2003, Jill and I decided we needed to go our separate ways. We were both sad about it. In the interest of pre-serving our deep friendship and continuing to nurture our two minor children, we parted amicably, even using the same lawyer. Jill is 20 years younger than I am. Maybe part of her view was similar to what I had felt when leaving the Dominicans and needed to take a stronger stance with regard to the life she felt she wanted and needed to live. Still, it hurt both of us deeply.

Once again I turned to writing to absorb the pain. I had already begun research on a book I hoped to write about Notre Dame. After borrowing a room from my good friend, Tim Carroll, I decided to get away from South Bend/Notre Dame so that I could do research and write. It was good therapy. I moved about 60 miles away to Valparaiso and rented an apartment in a nice complex. It was close enough that I could teach my classes, be with Trevor and Emily, the camp and Notre Dame Library within an hour. I stayed there for a year and completed my book. My son Jeremy had taken on part of the research, interviewing and writing and he initiated contact with Trace Murphy, an editor at Doubleday in New York. Trace pitched the idea of a book on Notre Dame and offered us a contract with a large advance against royalties. It was, in many ways, a dream come true. My whole life had been intimately connected to the University and its people and I finally would be able to attempt to distill and describe the spirit that permeated the place and its people. And I could do so under the Doubleday imprint.

As we prepared the final manuscript, it occurred to me that I should approach a prominent Notre Dame person to write a foreword to the book. A name came quickly to mind: a Notre Dame alumnus named Regis Philbin. I remembered what Tom Suddes had taught me years before, "Go ahead and ask; the worst that can happen is that you will get a No as your answer."

I was able to get Mr. Philbin's address and I sent him a letter with samples from the manuscript. One week later I received a response. Not only did he say Yes, he included his finished foreword! The book was published in September 2005. It received good reviews, but none as complimentary as this one by Bill Gunlocke in *America* magazine:

> The Lowells of Boston have nothings on these Langfords when it comes to institutional tradition. So who better to write about the place and call it, what else, *The Spirit of Notre Dame*?...As a compilation of viewpoints and memories, it reads like a Studs Terkel oral history. This is a book of voices, voices of people who went to Notre Dame or worked there, or felt for the place in some special way, even if they did not go there. *The Spirit of Notre Dame* is not only for Notre Dame alums, any more than *Rudy* is a movie for Domers alone. It is not even just for Catholics. It is a book about an American place that must mean enough to the country to have the only college football team whose every game is broadcast on national television.

No doubt my book was one of the reasons I was invited in 1997 to be a Hesburgh Lecturer in the program of the Notre Dame Alumni Association. It was a true compliment because they selected the best teachers to go to the more than 270 Alumni Association Clubs around the country, and to lecture on important topics. It was part of Notre Dame's initiative in continuing education for alumni.

An annual catalog listed all the lecturers and topics. I offered the "Church and Science," then added "Children of Poverty" and later added "The Spirit of Notre Dame" as my presentations. Over time I delivered some 24 talks to clubs in 15 states. Not that I needed any further evidence that our University turned out people of character, but I was amazed by the work these clubs did in their local communities. They had learned to serve at Notre Dame and they had not forgotten. I am still in touch with people from some of the clubs I visited 12 years or more ago.

I was also invited over the years to speak to various organizations such as Kiwanis, Lions, Boys and Girls Clubs, and more, on the stories and needs of the children at our camp.

I accepted an invitation to testify at a Congressional hearing on the state of the humanities in the United States. Needless to say I urged more, not less, support. But my most memorable talk was in Mexico City where I was to represent the United States publishing industry at an international symposium on the present and future of book publishing. The talk had to be given in Spanish. I wrote it in English, dusted off my Spanish and then gave it to Jose Anadon of the Notre Dame faculty to correct and polish.

It was great to see Mexico City again. I was nervous as I entered the auditorium. My accent is pretty good and, after a flattering introduction by the Mexican novelist Arturo Azuela, I vowed to rise to the occasion.

The talk seemed to be well received. But then I was

caught by surprise; the four main presenters were now asked to form a panel and to take questions from the audience. It was one thing to read a talk in a foreign language, but quite another to understand questions asked by native speakers or answering them fluently. I was trapped.

I did my best to understand and answer the questions directed to me; my answers were short and simple. On questions to the other presenters, I laughed when they did, nodded assent frequently and smiled a lot. Perhaps David Susskind had been right; maybe I should have been an actor. All I remember is how relieved I was when it ended.

My final Hesburgh Lecture was in 2010 at the Recognition dinner for all Hesburgh lecturers. It was somewhat daunting to speak before such an august audience. That made it even more special when they received my talk with a standing ovation. Karen Conway, Director of the lecture series, sent a CD of the talk to Father and he responded with this letter:

UNIVERSITY OF
NOTRE DAME

REV. THEODORE M. HESBURGH, C.S.C.

President Emeritus

1315 Hesburgh Library
Notre Dame, Indiana
46556-5629 USA

tel (574) 631-6882
fax (574) 631-6877
email Theodore.M.Hesburgh.1@nd.edu

February 12, 2010

Karen Conway
Alumni Association
100 Eck Center
Notre Dame, IN 46556

Dear Karen,

Thank you for sending me a copy of Jim Langford's keynote address from the Hesburgh Lecture Recognition Dinner.

It was certainly a wonderful lecture by Jim. He has played such an important role in the lecture series and I know everyone wishes him the very best.

My continued prayers and blessings for Jim and the work of the Alumni Association.

Ever devotedly in Notre Dame,

(Rev.) Theodore M. Hesburgh, C.S.C.
President Emeritus

In *The Spirit of Notre Dame*, I wrote a thank you to all the volunteers who ever served the children at TACH:

> To the hundreds and hundreds of Notre Dame students who have bicycled through the nine acres of woods, or played baseball, volleyball, basketball with the children, or joined them in the clubhouse for art and games, or the theater building for an impromptu talent show, or the sandbox with shovels and imagination, you embody the true spirit of Notre Dame. The children may not know all of your names, but God and his Mother, Notre Dame, surely do.
>
> You have seen and sensed how much these children cherish their time with you. You have heard some of their stories, and I have seen tears well up in your eyes as you try to retell them. Abuse and neglect, fear and anger should not be the daily bread of childhood.
>
> And I know that you sometimes feel like throwing stones toward heaven as if to awaken God, demanding to know how a just and loving God could let these things happen to children. But to ask the question is to risk having the same question asked of us, how could we let these things happen to children? In our own way, playing with the children, teaching by example, affirming their smiles and talents, just being available to them, we are the hands and the heart of the body of Christ on earth. Someone told me once that what we do is nice, but it is only a bandage, not a systemic cure. I responded that if you're bleeding a bandage comes first; the systemic cure comes later.
>
> I have watched you, sons and daughters of Notre Dame, over these years with more appreciation and inspiration than I could ever express to you.

I have seen you work minor miracles, seen your love and goodness bring grace in the form of smiles, as well as in changed demeanor in these children. They are so hungry for the presence you bring them.

Some of you actually changed your majors and life plans because of your experience at TACH. And you never had to secularize your motivation as you told others about the camp. A perfect case in point: One of you applied to Harvard Law School by saying he is a believing Roman Catholic and that this is what led him to TACH. His application then recounted this experience:

"I don't cry much. It's not that I don't feel deeply. Actually, most who are close to me would probably say the opposite is true. Maybe it's because I'm an ex-football player or because events over the years have upped the emotional quota that has to be reached before tears can fall. I just don't tend to cry a lot. But one April night during my junior year at Notre Dame, I wept.

"While at Notre Dame I was privileged to work with at-risk kids at a wonderful place called There Are Children Here. This proved to be a source of some of my most amazing experiences at Notre Dame. One weekend I was given the opportunity to work with kids from the projects in Chicago. Although I had already spent time with children from comparable situations in South Bend, I was not prepared emotionally for this experience. One little girl in particular stole my heart. She was a fifth-grader from a single parent family. She loved basketball, worked very hard in school, and had inquiring brown eyes. I remember hiding with her during a round of night-time hide and seek. We had the chance to talk and look at the stars. I was inspired by her words and sweet disposition, her positive attitude and strength of character. You couldn't help but love her.

"'Later I couldn't help wondering how many of these children would break out of their troubled circumstances. As a volunteer at TACH, you hope they all will. But this child enlarged that hope. More than ever, I wanted her to have a chance to make it.

"She cried when she said goodbye. She forced a smile between her tears and boarded a van back to Chicago. I was left standing there feeling overwhelmed. Later, in my room, I finally let go. It was then that I cried.

"I consoled myself that someday I will do more about this. How could life ever change for kids like her? Maybe it was a lost cause. I refuse to believe that. I want to right the wrongs. I want to effect change. I want my life to make a difference."

Others have written to say that, in retrospect, TACH was the best part of their Notre Dame education. If so, it is only because you made it so. You are the ones who grew in mind and heart and brought the gifts of intelligence and grace with you to TACH. William James once wrote that "the greatest use in life is spending yourself in something that will outlast you." How wonderful it is that by the time you leave Notre Dame you will have already done that.

—11—

Happiness

In retrospect, what TACH awoke in me is a spiritual dimension I had never known before, at least not to this degree.

I, who had lived in a religious community for ten years and failed, who had been in two marriages and failed twice, uncovered the grace that let me rise to the surface and breathe again. The camp taught me how to pray, it taught me how to care more for others than I ever thought possible, it taught me the meaning of courage and how to inspire others by welcoming their inspiration in return.

I never made a point of broadcasting the principles that motivated TACH, but I never hid them either. Sometimes one of the children would ask, "Why do you do this?" And it would give me a chance to say

"Because the Gospel tells us to love one another, to feed, clothe, comfort and visit each other. I hope you will volunteer to help others for the same reason."

My days of measuring beliefs and performance in the traditional way I had been taught were over. Dogma and orthodoxy were still in the room, but in the back row. Happiness demands and deserves more than just keeping the rules. The Beatitudes go beyond the rules and can bring truth in ways that obey and embody the Commandments. The issue becomes one of happiness, not just eternal, but in this life as well.

Happiness is easy to describe, but difficult to define. The desire for happiness is what moves and motivates us; it is a goal and a goad; it is our holy grail, our pearl of great price. But it also seems to be elusive, partial and fleeting. Why is something so central to human life so hard to identify, seek and possess? Its sources and trademarks ought to be clear, well known and beyond debate; but such is not the case. We are free to seek it where we will and to choose among the competing guiding signs along the way.

More than 300 years B.C. Aristotle noted the irony that something so basic in life as the heart of happiness should be subject to the allure of false pretenders, detours and dead ends. For him the ultimate goal of human life is happiness and we are obliged to search for true happiness and then to seek it with all our might. But how do we know where to find it?

The imposters that promise happiness are powerful. St. Thomas Aquinas admitted their seductiveness even as he pinpointed the limitations that mark them as pretenders. What object or activity can bring the fullness of lasting happiness? Some say wealth or pleasure of the senses. Others see power, fame or honors as the good that promises them their greatest chance at happiness.? Aquinas argued that the goods we find in the world can truly be wonderful, but that not one, or even all combined, can exhaust our desire to know and love without limit.

"Limitless" is the key word here. Created things, hemmed in by finite borders and fragility, cannot guarantee more than a taste of what unbounded happiness might be like. That taste serves to whet our appetite for more. St. Augustine, who plumbed every possible source of happiness, concluded that only God would do: "You have made us for yourself and our hearts are restless until they find their rest in you."

Money, sex, power and drugs continue to lure us and we continue to succumb. Even if we mortgage our spirit and barter away our self-respect, the end result is never enough, never enduring, and we are forced to give up what remains of our dwindling souls to try for more.

Real happiness, as distinguished from mere satisfaction, doesn't come easily. One clear day does not prove that spring is here; one good deed is not enough to make a person good — or happy. It takes an unshakable resolution, built on something that is worth living for — and dying for — to command the daily practice that is necessary to build the virtues, the habits that make doing good our second nature. Virtue is not a pet that comes when called. Wishing for it does not make it ours. Working for it does.

This is crucial because only the concert of virtues can make us free enough to be truly happy. Aristotle taught that happiness belongs more to the mind than to the will, that it is more a state of mind than a mode of operation. If he is right, then our very lifestyle can offer more hurdles than help on the way to happiness. Constant excitation of the senses may lessen boredom, but it also distracts us from the quiet we need to communicate with our inner selves. If we fall into the habit of sliding from one moment or one day to the next without reflection, our self-definition will be mainly a collection of loosely tied snapshots of reality.

The inability to be alone with oneself makes the quest for genuine and lasting happiness a mission impossible. Just as we cannot really love another until we love ourselves, neither can we hear others until we have listened to ourselves. We are all sinners; we all fail and fall; that's why happiness requires faith and hope. We have to get up and go on. We need to count on both justice and mercy. R.C. Lewontin makes this point beautifully:

> According to a Haggadic legend, when God decided to create the world he said to Justice, "Go and rule the earth which I am about to create." But it did not work. God tried seven times to create a world ruled by Justice, but they were all failures and had to be destroyed. Finally, on the eighth try, God called in Mercy and said, "Go, and together with Justice, rule

the world that I am about to create, because a world
ruled only by Justice cannot exist." This time, apparently it worked, more or less.

We cannot achieve perfect happiness in this life because perfect would require the quality of permanence,
of never ending. We have all had moments that caused
us to wish that this moment "could last forever."

Those moments are finite foretastes of what eternal, perfect happiness must be like. Time has to yield
to eternity to freeze the "now" so it can never change.
But the more we acquire virtue and see with the eyes
of faith, the more we can experience and relish the
experience of ecstasy, and the more happy we can be.

I knew happiness when I was a Dominican, in my
publishing work, writing, marriages and parenthood.
But none of those experiences could rival the happiness
I discovered working on a daily basis with the children
and volunteers at TACH. Those were and will always
be the happiest years of my life. And I know the reason
this is so. It is simply the paradox that you must lose
yourself to find yourself, and empty yourself to be
filled with joy. In the Sermon on the Mount, Jesus made
clear what spirit should animate those who would follow him. Tradition calls these teachings the Beatitudes
since they convey the promise of happiness:

> How happy are the poor in spirit:
> theirs is the kingdom of heaven.
> Happy the gentle:
> they shall have the earth for their heritage.
> Happy those who mourn:
> they shall be comforted.

Happy those who hunger and thirst for
  what is right:
they shall be satisfied.
Happy the merciful:
they shall have mercy shown them.
Happy the pure in heart:
they shall see God.
Happy the peacemakers:
they shall be called sons of God.
Happy those who are persecuted in the cause of
  right: theirs is the kingdom of heaven.

(5:3-10 *Jerusalem Bible*)

Put that together with the Gospel of St. Matthew
25:35-40):

"...for I was hungry and you gave me food. I was
thirsty and you gave me something to drink. I was a
stranger and you welcomed me, I was naked and you
gave me clothing, I was sick and you took care of me,
I was in prison and you visited me."

Then the righteous will answer him, "Lord, when
was it that we saw you hungry and gave you food, or
thirsty and gave you something to drink? And when
was it that we saw you as a stranger and welcomed
you or naked and gave you clothing? And when was
it that we saw you sick or in prison and visited you?"
And the King will answer them, "Truly I tell you, just
as you did it to one of these who are members of my
family, you did it to me."

I am certain that my years studying, praying and
meditating in the Dominicans really prepared me to
recognize happiness when it was actually in my grasp.
The whole TACH experience lit my soul, rekindled

my zeal, and fed my understanding of what real happiness feels like. No other human experience could match that. Among the miracles that I recognized at TACH was the fact that during all the years and the thousands of visitors and volunteers who spent time there, not a single incident of impropriety ever happened. As the revelations of clergy abuse became common, our camp remained uncommon.

Like many people, I am disheartened by the fact that our nation, perhaps our world, has seemingly gone in the opposite direction from the one predicted by Teilhard de Chardin. We are not closer. We are splintered, separated and afraid. Our young are bored. If this is all there is to life, get what you can any way you can. The German philosopher Friedrick Nietzsche detested Christianity precisely because it taught that you need to pick up your wounded and bring them along; the strong must take care of the weak. The mood today among too many people seems to favor Nietzsche. Listen to discussions about welfare, food stamps, school-lunch help for poor children, Head-Start programs, immigrants, the homeless, the elderly. And many televangelists simply make it worse as they rail on the unfortunate in order to raise more money for their coffers.

But sometimes we need to see the bottom of the barrel in order to be struck by how empty it is, and then to search afresh for answers that might stir us back to sanity and hope and love of one another. It is never too late to get back to the search.

—12—

Love Thee Notre Dame

─────────

I have already recounted some of my history at, and with, the University of Notre Dame, but I have not yet attempted to verbalize what this place and its people have meant to my life and my soul. As a child some of my happiest memories were of going to campus with my dad, especially during the war years when I was only four to eight years old.

I don't know how many of us are left who actually saw the marching of Navy ensigns in their navy blue uniforms on what is now the south quad. The flag raising was inspiring.

It was the Navy who saved Notre Dame from having to close as students were volunteering or being drafted into the armed forces. By selecting Notre Dame as one of the institutions of higher education that would be used to educate and train men for their positions as officers, the Navy sent enough students to keep the University alive. Reserve Officer Training is still a part of Notre Dame and there are memorials on campus honoring Notre Dame men who served in the armed forces. (My brother Walter was in the Air Force ROTC at ND and graduated in 1955 as a second lieutenant in the Air Force, from which he retired as a Lt. Colonel.)

After the war was won, at a convocation in the Navy Drill Hall, the University conferred an honorary degree on Admiral Chester Nimitz.

He concluded his acceptance talk by saying to the president of Notre Dame: "Father O'Donnell, you sent forth to me, as to other naval commands on every ocean and continent, men who had become imbued with more than the mechanical knowledge of warfare. Somehow, in the crowded hours of their preparation for the grim business of war, they absorbed not only Notre Dame traditional fighting spirit, but the spiritual strength too that this University imparts to all, regardless of creed, who come under its influence."

Scores of World War II veterans returned to campus to complete their studies for degrees. Many of them were married, so a small town, Vetville, grew on campus to house them. A recently ordained priest, Father Theodore M. Hesburgh, was a chaplain to the Vetville community.

Another iconic story emerging from the war years: The year was 1937; the scene, Notre Dame Stadium;

the game, a typical battle between Notre Dame and Southern California. Tied, 6-6 in the fourth quarter and deep in their own territory, the Irish call for a hand-off to number 58, Mario "Motts" Tonelli. He races for 70 yards to the USC 15-yard line. Three plays later, he scores the winning touchdown.

Tonelli had his class ring engraved with his initials, MGT, and his year of graduation, '39. He played one season with the Chicago Cardinals before joining the army in 1941 and being assigned to the Philippines. Then came December 7, 1941 and Pearl Harbor. Sgt. Tonelli, along with American and Filipino troops, received orders to retreat to the Bataan Peninsula to await reinforcements. The reinforcements never came, but the Japanese army did. And so began one of the most infamous and barbaric events in modern history, the 65-mile Bataan Death March. Food and water were scarce; anyone who fell or stopped would be killed by bayonet.

At one point, a guard spotted Tonelli's ring and demanded that he hand it over. With his life at risk, he gave it over. Before long, a Japanese officer approached him and asked whether one of his men had taken something from him. He said, "My ring." The officer put the ring in Tonelli's hand and said, "Keep it hidden." He added that he had graduated from USC and that he had seen Tonelli's touchdown in the 1937 game. "I know what this ring means to you," he said.

Some 11,000 prisoners died on the march. That was only the beginning. Over the next two and a half years of imprisonment and forced labor, there were beatings, starvation, and humiliation enough to break most human spirits. But Tonelli's ring always reminded him to hope. In 1944, now a mere 100 pounds, Tonelli was part of a group shipped to mainland Japan for slave labor. On arrival, he worked his way to the intake table to receive his identification number and prisoner clothes. The number assigned to him was 58, the same number he had worn on his Notre Dame jersey. He said later, "That's when I knew I'd make it."

Back in the U.S., he suited up with the Cardinals for a game against Green Bay. He soon decided to forego football in favor of public service in Chicago. He kept the ring with him always; it had survived horror as had he. Every day until his death on January 8, 2003, Mario Tonelli saw his survival as a victory and his Notre Dame ring as its trophy.

Stories like this abound at Notre Dame. In the wake of the devastating fire that burned down most of the campus in 1879, when the school had been in existence for only 37 years, Father Edward Sorin, CSC, the founder, was summoned home from Montreal to survey the tragic remains of his dreams. He gathered the community into Sacred Heart Church, one of the few buildings still remaining, and told them it was probably his fault for building the place too small and he promised we would build it bigger this time. "If it were all gone, I would not give up."

That is the spirit that still lives here. One does not have to memorize the line, it echoes generation after generation at this place and in its people.

As I advanced in my teen years, I had several different jobs on campus: I worked in the mimeograph shop, delivered mail in the main building, cleaned the stoves and ovens at the Morris Inn, and did occasional work at the Notre Dame Bookstore. The last two summers I was home, I worked as a tour guide on campus.. That was a great job. I could tell the story of Notre Dame and show people around the place I loved. All of this gave me a head start on the book I finally, almost a half century later, wrote. Perhaps I should have titled it *Stories of Notre Dame*.

I think much of the essential spirit and progress of Notre Dame can be traced to two men, each in his own way, founders of the University: Fr. Edward Sorin and Fr. Theodore M. Hesburgh.

When Father Sorin and seven brothers of Holy Cross reached the land given them in Northern Indiana, it was February 26, 1842. None of them could have imagined what this land would host in the decades ahead. A large man with dark skin and brooding eyes, Sorin was an imposing figure with an equally imposing faith and sense of divine mission. At just twenty-eight years old, barely speaking English, he was a recently ordained priest in a fledgling religious order, a man who embraced America as the place and path leading to salvation. By all accounts, he was well ahead of his years: bold, confident, shrewd, practical and on fire with faith in God and his fellow human beings. He emanated and embodied a spirit that drew and sustained followers.

The school he started began as a grade school and

trade school. Yet two years later he had the State of Indiana issue a charter for Notre Dame as a university. There is that optimism, born of faith and hope, dreaming big and working steadily.

The Holy Cross community at Notre Dame and its sister school, St. Mary's College, sent many priests and nuns to serve as chaplains and nurses during the Civil War. The most famous was Father William Corby, chaplain of the famed Irish Brigade; a statue of him blessing the troops as they prepared for battle is prominent at Gettysburg. And a perfect copy graces the Notre Dame campus in front of Corby Hall.

Growth in faculty, students and facilities was slow but steady. Until football. The early years, 1887 through 1899, claimed a modest record of 34 wins, 15 losses and 4 ties. But as the game gained popularity, so did the Fighting Irish. They came of age under Coach Jesse Harper and started beating strong competition. On November 1, 1913, the underdogs from South Bend beat powerhouse Army at West Point 35-13. Gus Dorias and Knute Rockne were the stars. The media took note. Catholic immigrants all over the country, but especially on the East Coast, began to identify with the small Midwestern Catholic school. The Irish, Italians, Eastern Europeans who had been buffeted by prejudice and disdain, now had someone to cheer for, someone who was besting the haters.

People started thinking that Notre Dame was where they wanted to send their sons.

After graduation, a loyal son, Knute Rockne, joined

the faculty as a chemistry teacher. In 1918, he was asked to replace Coach Harper. He said yes. In the next 13 years, from 1918-1931, Rockne's squads went 105-12-5 on the won, loss, tie scale and in the process they won five national championships. A plane crash in Kansas on March 31, 1931, took Rockne's life, but nothing could steal his legacy. As a teacher, coach, motivator and person, he embodied what was best about Notre Dame. His funeral, held at Sacred Heart Church on campus, the same place Father Sorin had spoken his inspired words after the fire in 1879, drew CBS to provide a national broadcast of the Mass and eulogy. Along with Babe Ruth, Knute Rockne was the sports celebrity of his time.

I don't intend to dwell here on the history of Notre Dame football. My point is simply to trace the development of a spirit that is intangible but real, a spirit I have seen, felt and experienced my whole life. It manifests itself in so many ways.

Is there something qualitatively different about the spirit at Notre Dame and good spirit displayed elsewhere? Perhaps. If so, it is to be found in the consistent pursuit of excellence at Notre Dame. Of course, there are failures, lapses, tragedies. But a failure, a lapse, a tragedy, needs to be admitted and corrected whenever possible. Falling short does not render invalid or defeat the resolve to continue seeking, nor the promise to find, keep, and nurture excellence.

If there is an ongoing battle between good and evil inherent in the human condition and patently evident in the flow of history, the Notre Dame I know comes down definitively on the side of goodness. Our failures and faults draw media like sharks to blood. If you proclaim the goal of excellence, your every misstep will be monitored and your failures, not your goodness, will be magnified. What I object to is not media coverage per se, it is the implication that somehow we are no longer eligible to be included on the list of communities devoted to excellence.

I have witnessed and admired Notre Dame's continuing quest. **I sensed it** in the students I taught over 23 years. The vast majority of them were from upper middle-class families; they easily could have adopted the badges of privilege. Instead, they embrace serving the less fortunate people living in the area of the South Bend community. I have already described the wonderful steady volunteer stints they logged at There Are Children Here. But you cannot name a single non-profit program in the area that does not benefit from the service of Notre Dame students. It is more than impressive; it is a sign of something greater than that. I see it as a result of a spirit, a grace, being accepted and passed along to others. Friendships are formed here that last a lifetime. The word I am looking for to describe the attitude of student volunteers is "compassion."

I sensed it in the faculty and their dedication not only to research and writing, but also in their commitment to good teaching, mentoring and caring. I knew many of them as teaching colleagues and as authors of books for the Notre Dame Press. What impressed me most was how happy most of them seemed. There was a strong, widespread, positive attitude that far exceeded the sour attitude of negative critics who, likely, would not be happy anywhere. The faculty here are proud to be here. I gained inspiration from people like Jay Brandenberger, Charles Wilber, George Howard, Bob Schmuhl, Tom Swartz and many others.

I sensed it in the administrators and staff that work here, whether as president or in maintenance, mail delivery or groundskeeping. There is a feeling of loyalty that you sense just being around the place. People here take pride in their work. I think of Fr. Ferd Brown, Pat Holmes, Roger Schmitz, Kathleen Cannon, Ava Preacher, Al Neiman, Steve Fredman, Don Costello and many more.

I sensed it in the alumni and alumnae of Notre Dame. As a Hesburgh Lecturer, I traveled to 16 states, some two or three times, to speak to Notre Dame clubs. And what I saw was the dedication, diligence, kindness and hard work they took with them from Notre Dame to bring to their local communities. "Impressive" doesn't cover it; but "excellence" does.

I have not been everywhere in the world, so, logically I cannot induce the statement that this is the best community anywhere. But I can enumerate the attributes of the people here and deduce that they add up to something well beyond the ordinary.

There are 275 Notre Dame Alumni Clubs around the world. They thrive because graduates want to stay in touch with the University and with each other. They do more than meet. They act. One example: is the N.D. Club of Gettysburg, PA. They have been involved in the Manos Unidos organization in Gettysburg, supplied 1,850 articles of new clothing to servicemen and women at Landstuhl Hospital, worked to clean the roadsides on the routes into Gettysburg, sponsored lectures and retreats and on and on. I had the pleasure of speaking there some years ago and I have never forgotten these good people, especially Jim Conrad.

I sensed it as I walk around campus. You can touch the bricks made by the brothers more than 170 years ago, visit the Log Chapel where Knute Rockne was baptized, see the humble first college building, still standing and in use today. This place has a history that is always in touch with the present. Fr. Hesburgh once said that if you want to know what makes this place work, look up to the Lady on the Dome. Seeped in history and at the forefront of research and the growth of knowledge and its uses, this place can renew one's soul. I know. It has done so for me many times.

Father Bill Seetch said it better, and more concisely than I can. Talking about what makes Notre Dame a different kind of place, he noted

> Those fortunate enough to come here are not merely fed, they are nourished. Mentally, physically, emotionally and spiritually we are nourished. The totality of one's personhood is attended to here. Few places in the world do that.
>
> This to me is the essence of the Notre Dame spirit. It is not athletics or the greatest fight song ever written.

It is the nourishment received that keeps us coming
back. We fill our tanks when we visit so we can leave
refreshed, renewed and recharged.

Let me add this: Mary stands now, as she has for
150 years, atop the Dome, a sign of care and hope in a
world desperate for both. There is always work to be
done; excellence is never owned. I love Notre Dame
because I know it to be a beacon of light, an explorer
and transmitter of truth discovered the hard way—by
study and prayer—and a font of grace that reaches out
to touch the nooks and crannies of the world.

The spirit of Notre Dame also is a legacy of Father
Theodore Hesburgh who was its president from 1952-
1987. I cannot add anything to the universal outpour-
ing of appreciation in the wake of his death on
February 26, 2015. Appointed by Presidents and
Popes, admired by a multitude of people who met him
in one place or another along his 20-million-mile journey around this world. More than anyone in American Catholic history, he was the Catholic Church in
America at its best.

Father Sorin had dreamed of starting a school.
Father Hesburgh envisioned and worked to build the
greatest Catholic university in history. He brought back
knowledge and reports and insights from everywhere
he went. He was a citizen of the world. He was cosmo-
politan in his openness to people, ideas and faiths. Sev-
en hundred years ago, when St. Thomas Aquinas was
attacked for having based much of his philosophy on
the work of Aristotle, a pagan, Aquinas replied: "Take
whatever is good and true, no matter the source."

Father Hesburgh was able to be away from campus precisely because his managerial principle was to put good and talented people in positions of authority and let them do their jobs. When he was on campus and working late in his office on the third floor of the Administration or Main Building, students would climb the fire escape and tap at his window. He would invite them in and listen to their ideas, requests, or confession. Though he served in the halls of power such as Washington, D.C. or the Vatican, he was fully at ease talking with *campesinos* in Chile or the residents at the Center for the Homeless in South Bend. He once said: "The very essence of leadership is that you have to have a vision. It has to be a vision you articulate clearly and forcefully on every occasion. You can't blow an uncertain trumpet." The vision he had, the note he played, did not vacillate or vary.

My parents were among his close friends. Father Ted had asked them to lead the first Peace Corps group to Chile in 1961; he visited them as often as he could and traveled up and down the long coast with my dad visiting the Peace Corps projects and volunteers, most of whom were from Notre Dame. It was Father Ted who also called on my parents ten years later to become Director of the Gulf and Western Foundation in the Dominican Republic where their job would be to bring aid to those suffering from hunger, disease and despair. My mother suffered a stroke and died in Santo Domingo in 1975 and my Dad lived until 2001.

Father Hesburgh presided over and preached at their funerals at Sacred Heart Church on campus.

Were I to try to sum up Father Ted's philosophy, I would do so by utilizing Aristotle's schema of the four causes:

The material cause is the stuff out of which things are made.

The formal cause is the direction the internal force gives to the matter.

The efficient cause is what caused it in the first place.

The final cause is what its goal is. This is the most important of the causes. It asks, "what is it for?" Father Hesburgh's answer would be "excellence" as the culmination of all human ventures. We seek excellence. And if we fall short, we get up and keep moving on the path to it. His like will not pass our way again.

When I was writing my book about Notre Dame, I penned an ode to the place. Trace Murphy, my editor at Doubleday, thought it was "a bit over the top." He might have been right. But this memoir is my last chance to post it. It is a love letter. It reads:

NOTRE DAME IS....

Home. A place where young spirits and hope soar,
and hope flames brightly
on faces and in hearts,
where consolation and healing await the weary,
a place where sorrow and self doubt, failure and loss can
be brought to the railing at the Grotto and entrusted to the
Lady who stands watch over all who come there.

A Holy Site to people who never lived here or studied here, but in some real and mysterious way, let it have a place in their life. For some, it is a sign, a goal, a tabernacle, a favorite place (even though unvisited), a destination. For Catholics, it stands as proof of a coming of age in America, against the odds, in the face of intolerance, with no diminishment of faith.

A Font of Grace. Almost as if it is a field of favor, this place takes hold, sometimes even of the most recalcitrant, and removes the scales from eyes so they can see again—or maybe for the first time—with the vision of faith. Miracles happen here—little ones and big ones—insights, decisions, acceptance, rejuvenation, teased out by some power that reaches the mind and soul. Hardness of heart finds no easy home here; magnanimity, bigness of soul, is in the land and landscape. The graves of the unsung heroes who built the place, brick by brick, who cleaned and baked, cooked and cared, are nearby and somehow the spirit of giving all for the common good is in the air breathed here, a legacy that emanates from those who were here before us and that, with our touches added, will be here for those who come after us, for all time.

Classrooms with a crucifix on the wall, a silent reminder that knowledge and truth need to culminate in goodness. Preparation for life, not simply for a profession, happens here; there is no such thing as Catholic chemistry, but there is such a thing as a worldview that sees all of nature through eyes of faith and so catches nuances and tones that do not distort the picture; they simply make it whole.

People, generation after generations of them, here to study, write, teach, pray, work; privileged to be in the company of other searchers in a place dedicated to Mary, the mother of Jesus. It is a family and it can trace its immediate lineage back to 1842, and its real ancestry back more than two millennia. Like every family, it has its share of dysfunction. Unlike every family it also has the resources and the will to act in the best interest of the individual and the community as a whole. It is possible that there is no place on earth with a greater concentration of good people. No one who comes here seeking solace, inspiration, knowledge or care leaves unchanged. Like it or not, sense it or not, to come here is to be touched by and to take away some portion of the grace that seems to spring from the very ground. Not to worry; the supply is infinite.

Memories shared by alumni, staff, and faculty, active and emeriti, of friends and friendships, of dorm life and homesickness, of dances and pep rallies, of the lakes and the lights on the Dome, of Masses that uplifted, teachers who inspired, of talks long and deep that probed the very mystery of life. Physical presence here might now seem only a snapshot in time, like the photos of the south quad filled with the formation of men in uniform training for battle during World War II, or earlier, the pictures of young men standing on campus next to unicycles brought back from Europe by Father Sorin. The spots where they stood are still there, still identifiable. You can still stand where Knute Rockne did when he was baptized in the Log Chapel on November 20, 1925. Or where his casket rested in Sacred Heart Church.

Some day people will look at images of those on campus now and pause for a moment to marvel not at the changes, but at the continuity. No one who has ever walked near the Dome at night will forget how little and how large it made them feel just to be there. The statue of Father Sorin faces toward Notre Dame Avenue so that he can welcome his sons and daughters home again.

—13—

Back to Publishing

Although I thoroughly enjoyed working with Psychology Professor George Howard on various projects for two years, I missed publishing. Jill had sold Diamond Communications to the Rowman and Littlefield Publishing Group, and, after stellar work at Loyola Press (including the acquiring and editing *The Gift of Peace* by Cardinal Bernardin), and working for Sheed and Ward in an effort to rebuild that Catholic iconic publishing house, Jeremy joined Jill in working for Rowman and Littlefield. Jill was in the Taylor Trade division and Jeremy was Director of Sheed and Ward, recently acquired by Rowman and Littlefield. I decided to see whether I could make it a trifecta. I contacted Jon Sisk, the able and amiable

219

Director of Publishing there. His response was prompt. They would be delighted to have me aboard as Consulting Editor. So, at one point there were three Langfords working for Rowman and Littlefield.

I have to say I really enjoyed working with Jon Sisk. Not only is he highly capable, he is highly personable as well. I was able to steer a number of great books to R and L, the most notable two books by Professor Alasdair MacIntyre who I think is the most important philosophical thinker of our time, and two by Fr. Nicholas Ayo, whom I regard as one of the very best spiritual writers of our time. But there were many more, as well, and I am proud to have played a role in their publication.

I left Rowman and Littlefield only because I had decided to start a publishing company. I broached the idea to my good friend, Tim Carroll, who had enjoyed a successful career in the print and production end of the business. When I learned that my successor at the University of Notre Dame Press had no plans to publish books about Notre Dame, its history or present, I saw it as a clear field, ready for cultivation and with a niche market that would be attentive to good books. Tim saw the potential and the challenge of the venture and agreed to co-found it with me. After careful consideration, we decided to name the company Corby Publishing, LP, in honor of Father William Corby, Chaplain of the Irish Brigade at Gettysburg, twice President of the University, and a man of courage and compassion. We incorporated in the State of Indiana in 2007 and set about to find projects that would live up to our motto: "Books That Make a Difference."

Our first book was titled *Creating Happy Memories: 101+ Ways to Create and Strengthen Family Ties*, by Pamela Ogren, with a foreword by Father Theodore M. Hesburgh. Corby was off and running, with a lot of help from our friends. Kerry Temple, editor of *Notre Dame Magazine*, alerted us to the remarkable photographic renderings of the Notre Dame campus by Matt Cashore, and suggested that we meet. Plans for an oversize, coffee-table, full-color book came together quickly. Kerry volunteered to write the text that would accompany the pictures. He suggested a friend, Noah Armstrong, to provide the internal design.

Tim asked Bob and Jim Priebe of Lithotone Printing in Elkhart, Indiana to work with us on setting payment terms for the printing job. Happily, they agreed. Even at that we were risking the house. Most small publishers (and some big ones) have to take risks like that. If we weren't in publishing, you'd likely find us at the casino or racetrack. You can make informed decisions, place your bet on how many you should print, how well it will sell and what the return versus cost might be. In my 45 years in the business, there are untold numbers of books in various warehouses along the way that I was sure would sell. I have to live with my mistakes and try not to picture the trees that were cut down to make the paper used up in printing.

On the other hand, there are thousands of books in the hands of people, or on their bookshelves, that I had a hand in bringing into print. And along the way, the vast majority of authors I worked with were grateful, pleasant and rightly proud of their work. Of course, some were difficult, unpleasant and overly proud of their work. That goes with the territory. Publishing brings you into contact with strong and sometimes egocentric people. Some appreciate all you do, others are never satisfied that you do enough.

Lots of things have changed in book publishing in the past two decades. The standard offset printing that was commonly used for print runs of one thousand or more copies is still available. But most printers are now relying on digital presses that are able to do a few or as many as 750 copies at a reasonable cost. These presses are used either for printing on-demand jobs or for short-run printing. The latter allows publishers, whether professional or self-publishers, the ability to print enough without needing a warehouse. As the book sells, it can go back to press quickly. The publisher is saved some risk by being able to order smaller quantities and also saved money by less expensive storage costs.

Although the national bookstores like Borders, Waldens, Daltons and others have gone the way of the dinosaur, small, niche bookstores are popping up to fill the gap. Even Barnes and Noble, having survived thus far, is closing instead of expanding its reach. That pretty much leaves it to the publisher's website to supply books. The big dog is now Amazon. com and, though I resisted selling through them for a while, I can now say that they are amazingly efficient. Authors who used to ask, "Will my book be advertised in the *New York Times*?" now want to know, "How soon will my book be available on Amazon?" The other consequence of this is that small publishers don't need a credit and collection department. Amazon pays.

I remember an author who, years ago, called me to complain that his second cousin had gone to the Barnes and Noble store in Waco, Texas and they did not have his book in stock. He wanted to know why this was so. I prayed for patience and pointed out that there are some 75,000 new titles published in the United States in any given year and that no bookstore could possibly stock more than 2% of those because they also had to stock fast-selling titles from the backlists. And, when the angel of patience had left the scene, I added, "It's somewhat unlikely that a bookstore in Waco would stock a book on the nuances of the early theories of Nicholas of Cusa. But," I told him, "your second cousin can order it directly from us."

Marketing and advertising have changed too. Print ads are not of much use anymore. They have been replaced by word-of-mouth, social media recommendations, blogs, Facebook, Google and Yahoo.

One advantage of all of this is that books have a longer life. The big chain stores used to give a new title a few weeks to a couple of months to sell enough to justify their space on the store shelves. Amazon has nearly three million titles for sale. And room for more.

Another change that drives new authors to smaller publishers or to self-publishing is that, with the consolidation of the large publishing houses in New York, new authors cannot really get a hearing without an agent and they can't get an agent without some evidence that he or she will have something they can sell to a large house for a healthy advance against royalties. I wonder whether William Faulkner could make it through the roadblocks today.

And finally, there is the competition coming from the less expensive ebooks. Younger readers who have not known the pleasure of turning paper pages or the feel and look of a well-made book or the smell of paper and print, are satisfied with the electronic versions. They are easier to carry on an airplane or in a car, and they don't need bookshelves in which to wait for someday extinction.

I'm an old-timer; I cherish books. They are friends. My close friends. But I try to stay abreast of the changes; several Corby titles have been made into ebooks.

Corby Publishing is now in its eighth year; to date we have published some 50 books. Except for Bessie Ross's summer internship, we have done all the work by ourselves.

We also relied on the advice and scouting of Father Nicholas Ayo, CSC, a member of the Notre Dame faculty. I had published several of his books at Notre Dame Press and two more at Rowman and Littlefield.

Fairly quickly, Corby Books began to make its mark. Books about Notre Dame were and are our main fare, but we also grew into fields such as Motivation, Spirituality, Current Issues and Academics.

Tim and I have put in countless hours over the years acquiring, preparing and publishing books that make a difference. It is a good thing we didn't go in expecting to make money. We look back with gratitude at the friendships we have made along the way.

—14—

Health Matters

I n the late spring of 2001, Jill, Trevor, Emily and I drove to Ft. Myers, Florida to visit Jill's Mom. We planned on staying a week or more. But after a few days, I was called home to deal with issues that needed my full and immediate attention. I planned to fly home, take care of business and fly back to Ft. Myers before driving the family home.

Tim Carroll picked me up at the airport and drove me home. I had felt some discomfort on the plane and again in the car, but I thought it was just some minor indigestion. When I got home, the discomfort turned into pain in my chest and down my arms so strong that the only relief I could find was to kneel by the bed, extend my arms out on it, and try to relax. I called my doctor, described what was happening and he referred me to a cardiologist and made the appointment for me ASAP.

The first thing he had me do was the stress test. I asked the nurse what the average time was to be on the equipment. She said about eight minutes. I lasted about 90 seconds and felt like a heart attack was about to happen. Test over. I flunked. More calls were made and I was given some pills, told I had to get my affairs in order so I could be hospitalized and prepared for surgery the next day. Josh was already on a flight from Chicago to Ft. Myers so that he could drive the family back non-stop. When they made it to the hospital, I could see their apprehension and their love. Jeremy drove over from Chicago, my sister Lois and her husband Bill were on hand. I was strangely calm. I had made my peace with God and the angels, been surrounded by my family with love, and I was ready to face whatever was next. My sons nicknamed me "the Hammer." The fact is that in the past two days I had spent every moment preparing to go to the other side. My conscience told me that I had been far from perfect—maybe only modestly good—but, like Cyrano de Bergerac, I had one thing that was totally unsullied, my white plume, and that was how I had cared for God's children. I fantasized that I would have with me a sheaf of notes and letters from the children we had cared for at the camp and that, plus their smiles, would be enough to get me through the golden gate. Jesus had said, "Unless you become like little children you shall not enter the kingdom." And he had instructed his apostles, "Let the children come to me." I wrote a prayer:

Lord, I need to talk with you about the children. I wonder why you keep sending them to us

You surely know how we treat them, what we do
       to them

You have taken so many of them back before they even
       owned a doll
          or dreamed of hitting a home run
          or thought about living long enough to graduate
          from high school.

We have let them die of random gunshots,
          starvation, drugs and disease,
          of loneliness, abuse and despair.

A friend who is a counselor at a local elementary school told me that
          in the past two weeks he has dealt with
          two suicide notes, three fifth graders who have
             joined a notorious gang,

and more than a few fifth graders who are sexually active.

What have we done...or not done...to your children?
          Who can they trust

What must you be suffering?

You, who still a child, amazed the elders in the temple.

You, who though exhausted at the end of a day of
          preaching and teaching,

Ordered your apostles not to prevent the children from
          coming to you.

And it was you, Lord, who told us that we need to become
          like children if we are to enter the kingdom.

I think what you meant was unless we speak
          the truth

Unless we trust and dream and hope and love
Unless we play and laugh and reach out to others
With both hands like children are meant to do
      we cannot be ready to see you.
Show us the way, Lord. Help us.

Of all the letters and notes I have received over the years from TACH campers, these are the two I hope to present as credentials:

> Dear Jim,
> I had lots of fun at camp. I had seen many things. I learned how to be nice to people. You are nice to talk to. You are fun. You are funny and you are a nice person. I want to thank you for the joy you brought into my life.
> Your friend,
> Porsha

> Dear Jim,
> How's life? How's the camp? How's my friend Trevor? Well I hope I can come back because I enjoyed myself. Thank you for having me come to the camp. I had fun with you and the kids from Notre Dame. I wish I could go over there to see you again. Please write back to me. I enjoyed myself with all the fun things. I miss you and your family. You have a good Easter you and your family. I enjoy hanging out with ya. I love ya. Tell everyone I said hello. Thank you for letting us play there and thank you for all you have done. Love you. Hope to see you again. Stay cool and nice, sweet, loving and caring person. I will pray for you if you need it. Love always,
> Toni

If these two don't help get me through the pearly gate, I'll bring the note from my friend at the Iowa mental hospital which certifies, "This guy is OK."

Back to my heart surgery. It was my good fortune to have as my surgeon Dr. Jim Kelly. Everyone agreed he was the best. The blockages were such that he had his work cut out for him. It turned out to be a sextuple bypass and the operation took nearly four hours. The anesthesiologist, Dr. Whipperman, a friend of Tim Carroll's told him later that my inside parts were in very good shape, to which Tim replied, "You must not have seen his liver."

As I regained consciousness in the recovery room, I was on a gurney which was then rolled into the hallway on the way to my room. I saw the beautiful faces of my family and became aware that I had made it; I was still here. A few days later it was time to go home. After two weeks, I was able to go down to the camp and see the children. No running, no batting, no basketball. Just smiles and banter. It was so good to be back.

Over the summer my heart and incision continued to heal rapidly. I discovered that you don't necessarily know that you have heart blockages; it's easy to attribute slowing down to age or workload. When it finally hits you and you get it cared for, your heart says thank you every day. I was ready to teach again and to do research with Professor Howard.

Seven years after the heart repair, I began having urinary problems, and pain, especially when I was on the riding mower cutting my acre of grass. It hurt enough that I called my doctor. He sent me to a urologist, Dr. Paul Toth who, in turn, sent me to Memorial Hospital for tests. They revealed that there was a growth on my bladder. They did a biopsy. When his nurse called to tell me that he needed to see me, I suspected the worst. Dr. Toth is modest in height, blunt in language and an expert at what he does.

We talked a bit and then he got down to business. "You have bladder cancer," he told me. I asked whether and how it could be treated. He waited for me to react. He repeated, "You have cancer." I replied "F**k cancer." I was not pretending to be John Wayne, that was my reaction in two words. I asked what treatment he recommended. He explained my options, gave me some pamphlets and said I should get surgery at the Indiana University in Indianapolis. His nurse made the call to Dr. Richard Foster's office there and I was told to register at the hospital in four days.

Time to summon the family for one more drama. Jeremy, Josh, Jill, Trevor and Emily came to Indianapolis to be with me before and after the surgery. With any kind of major surgery, there is always the risk of some unexpected complication arising. So it is well to say prayers, express love, and rely on hope.

The bladder, prostate and surrounding cells would be removed. There were two options to choose from in finding another way to store and excrete urine. The bladder, prostate and surrounding cells are removed, the surgeon can build a new bladder out of material from the intestine, a bladder that would be inside the body and which would operate in a way similar to the way the original bladder did. The other option is to create a stoma, again from intestinal material, which would remove urine from the body into a urostomy bag that is outside the body and serves as a reservoir, until emptied or replaced by a new bag. That is the option I chose. Had I been younger I would have opted for the internal bladder replacement, but the ostomy seemed less likely to cause future problems.

Although it is not difficult to get used to wearing and caring for an ostomy system, you always know it is there and that you need to take care of it. The important thing is that Dr. Foster was confident that all the cancer had been removed. Anytime I'm tempted to complain about the hassles of the ostomy bag I think how lucky I am to have survived cancer or to have been spared kidney problems.

Fast forward another two years. I am no longer teaching or working with Professor Howard. All my time is devoted to Corby Books. One half of my two-car garage warehouses our stock. I acquire the new books, negotiate the contracts, register the ISBNs, do the bookkeeping, compile and file the taxes, and manage accounts receivable. Tim handles freelancing the copy editing, designing the inside and cover of the books, shopping for the best prices and printing schedules and sharing the work of sending out review copies and managing large deliveries. We work well together.

It was late February and I was on my way from my garage to the mail box on the opposite side of the road. There was only a little snow on the ground but it was cold and the wind was strong, making it colder. As I was nearly to the road, I hit a patch of black ice, flew up in the air, and came down on the asphalt with my total weight. I knew instantly that it was bad. I tried to get up but the pain and my left leg and hip wouldn't allow me to raise myself. Since it was cold and there were no cars coming by, I had somehow to make it back to the garage. I crawled, dragging my leg like I had seen wounded soldiers do in movies. I made it to my car, pulled myself up to find my cell phone on the front seat and called Jill. I thought if she and her friends Rick and Doug could get me into the house and to my bed, I could assess the damage. They got me up and it was clear to them that my leg was broken. They called an ambulance.

A wild trip with needle jabs in the arm, a fast track past the emergency room, x-rays, and on to surgery performed by Dr. Stephen Mitros. The broken bone was very near where the leg connects to the hip. The next time I woke up the operation was declared a success. Let the healing begin!

After nearly a week, surviving on the kindness of relatives and friends who sneaked food and root beer in to me, I was assigned to the physical therapy department. I know it was necessary, but it sure wasn't fun. I came up with an appropriate nickname for my therapist: The Iron Maiden. I gained strength and kept asking when I might be released. The physical therapist told the head doctor that I should stay another week. I was told that on a Friday. I let them know that I would not accept that and I planned to leave with their permission or not. The head man came to my room and told me that if I left without a release, Medicare would not cover my bill. I said, "I'll take another mortgage on my house; I'm getting out of here." He offered to compromise. We agreed that I would be released on Monday, not next Friday. They probably were delighted to see me go, but not half as happy as I was.

Jeremy and Josh bought me a wonderful Irish cane; Lois and Bill did my grocery shopping, Walter and Barb took care of me...life was good.

But a month later, when it seemed I was fine and all my help had gone back to their lives, I woke up one morning with my left leg bloated to twice its normal size. I think it was the most painful experience I ever had. I called my doctor, Dr. James Tieman, and he said for me to get to the hospital immediately. By now the ambulance people knew the way to my house by heart. These events made me sad. I had always prided myself on not needing medical attention more than a physical exam once a year.

This time I had deep vein thrombosis, a blood clot in the leg. The danger was that if even part of it broke loose and went to my lungs, I would be in serious trouble. Medication and special treatments safely dissolved the clot. But my heart had not liked the whole thing. One more trip to the operating room to have a pacemaker implanted. By now, the whole series of events began to seem ludicrous. As the surgeon and staff were preparing me for the implantation, there was a loud banging on the operating room door. I raised my head and said, "Would someone get that? It's my Jimmy Johns." Everybody laughed and then got on with the procedure. Two days later I was paroled and have not been back since.

—15—

The Beauties of Autumn

F all has always been my favorite season. The trees
are dressed in their colorful best, the breezes
become cooler, football season arrives, and the
year begins to wind down. Some great poets and es-
sayists have claimed that fall works as a metaphor for
life itself. I think it does. Before a leaf withers and dies,
it shows a brightness and beauty that crowns its life.
Before a light bulb gives out, it sends a burst of light as
if to say "I saved my brightest gift for last."

As this book might testify, my life, like that of most
everybody else, has been filled with both hits and errors. And now, in the fall of my life, I have been blessed
in a most unexpected way.

Since my divorce, I have lived alone for ten

years, maintained a deep friendship with Jill, helped my younger children grow and loved the quiet and privacy of my ranch home in the country. The thought of living or dying alone has never scared me. Perhaps it is a latent desire to stay far from the madding crowd, or maybe a spiritual longing learned in my Dominican days that silence and solitude feed my soul. I was not a hermit on Tyler Road. I enjoyed many friendships with students, authors, Cubs fans, and women with whom I have stayed in touch over the years, especially Nellie, Suzy, Louise, and Donna. But nothing and no one could really budge me from my retreat, except, of course, the kids until There Are Children Here had to close.

And then, as Providence would have it, I had a phone call from my sister Lois about a friend of hers who had just self-published a book about her life. I said I'd be happy to read it and help her any way I could. The book, *Come This Way: There Is an Exit* by Nimbilasha Cushing, touched my heart and caught me with the writing ability of its author. Her story told of being born in St. Louis, and, after her mother died, being sent to Tennessee to be raised by grandparents, who were sharecroppers, then back to St. Louis and her father and a new stepmother, getting education whenever she could, relying on her faith always. Her exit from what might have been a dead end was to enlist in the Air Force. After her tour of duty, she became a flight attendant for United Airlines. Soon she was assigned exclusively to trans-oceanic flights. She retired after 31 years as a flight attendant. She had married a distinguished Professor at Notre Dame, but had now been a widow for some 10 years. I told Lois to have her call me if she wished. She did call and agreed to come to my home for a talk about publishing.

On April 3, 2012, when I saw her car in my driveway and saw her coming to the front door, my first impression was that she was very attractive, nicely attired and pleasant. Once she was seated in the living room, we exchanged pleasantries about my sister and talked a bit about her late husband, Jim Cushing, who I knew from having published one of his books at the University of Notre Dame Press.

Book talk took over at that point. We had a good conversation and she seemed open to learning everything she could about publishing. We vowed to stay in touch and we did so by email and phone. I signed off an email to her six days after we met: "I'll be glad for any occasion, professional or social, that affords me the opportunity to spend more time with you. You are a special person." It had not taken me long to discover that there is an extraordinary and totally genuine kindness about her; it is impossible not to like her.

By the end of June 2012, we had both fallen in love; I was first, she followed. I told her I was smitten with her. I think she liked the word "smitten." Our bond had grown quickly; we sat on a bench by one of the lakes at Notre Dame and she leaned her head into my arms. As you get older, cutting to the truth trumps long processes that consume precious time. I have no doubt that it was not Lois alone who led us to meet; there was some other angel involved as well.

Nimbi is a deeply spiritual person and she lives what she believes. She has a prayer partner by phone every morning. She told me one time that she was feeling disconnected from God. I offered some advice I read once: "Be of good spirit and joyful. If Jesus or you play hide-and-seek sometimes, the point is to trust that the looking, not necessarily the finding, is what really counts."

I want to tell an extended story that tells what it is like to be loved by Nimbi.

It happened more than 35 years ago. It was a moment; actually much more than a moment. The memory of it has not been dulled by time. I was in San Francisco to attend the annual meeting of the Association of American University Presses. One hundred fifty or so representatives from 72 presses spent a weekend listening to talks, sounding each other out on how to deal with the pressures of running a mostly deficit operation in the context of administrators more interested in budgets than publishing scholarly books. I normally did not like to attend these meetings but the lure of San Francisco took me to this one.

On Saturday evening, there was a cocktail party for all attendees. I was talking with the Director of Texas A and M Press when we both went silent, our attention captured by one of the most beautiful women we had ever seen. She was Asian, Japanese, as I later discovered, and her smile and attitude announced that she was much more than her beauty. I went over and introduced myself. We began a conversation and quickly found common ground. Quietly we slipped away from the party and went to the hotel bar. We took a booth. As the evening wore on, we built a bond. We really liked each other. I think we were there for hours. Her name was Kathleen Matsueda and she told me she would soon be giving up her job at the University of Hawaii Press and returning to Japan.

To be honest, I was tempted to conceal my recent engagement to Jill and to spend as much time with her as I could, but our bond was more spiritual than physical. I told her I was engaged. We hugged and said good night.

Sunday morning was get-away day and my flight would leave about noon. I went down for an early breakfast and then back to my room to pack. There was a knock on my door. It was Kathleen. We both knew that there was some kind of magic between us. We talked, hugged a while, traded addresses and parted.

It was a beautiful experience, one I would never forget. I didn't ever sense how deeply embedded it was until Nimbi and I watched a movie, *Lost in Translation*, starring Bill Murray and Scarlett Johansson, about two people who meet and bond quickly, but due to other commitments, part without going further. They had a magic experience and chose to leave it that way.

Nimbi noticed my eyes water. I had experienced the story that movie told. It was one of the rare times I bowed to Plato instead of Aristotle and let love rise to a truly spiritual union, filled with goodness and purity, unhampered by anything that might weigh it down. I'm guessing more people have had a similar experience. Kathleen is my road not taken. How different would my life have been if I had spent it in another land with her?

Nimbi is the one who put it in perspective for me. She had seen the tears in my eyes as I watched the end of the movie. I had told her about my unique experiences with Kathleen. Nimbi said to me, "I saw your emotion. I just want you to know that she could not have loved you as much as I do." Those are the most loving words I have ever heard.

I have never known anyone as generous as she is with her time, energy, resources, and love. Lots of people say "I love you" to others, but Nimbi really means it. People call her, greet her, remember her because her words carry real affection and not just vowels and consonants. She is a Kiwanis member and a volunteer at most of their service tasks. She volunteers every week at the free clinic, the Christ Child Society, at the Habitat for Humanity Women's Build and at an assisted living home. She takes people to church, helps friends who need a favor, donates food and clothes on a regular basis, and she is devoted to her immediate and extended family in a way that puts me, and most of us, to shame. For good measure, she belongs to a writers group and a book club.

In August 2012 we decided to invite family and friends to a party celebrating our joyful relationship.

It was like a wedding; we professed our love to each other in front of a full house at Trios in downtown South Bend. We had decided not to have a formal church wedding in order to avoid having to revise our estates, file joint tax returns and so forth. But we needed to eliminate the almost daily 50-mile round trip between our houses. I decided to sell my home and move to Nimbi's. The only thing I worried about was how my cat would react. For the first 7 years of her life she was an indoor/outdoor cat. From now on she would be kept indoors. It has worked out perfectly. Nimbi has progressed from being a non-cat person to loving and caring for our pet.

It feels like we have been married for 30 years. We are comfortable together despite the fact that she is orderly and I am not. We share menu planning and cooking. Nimbi has been really helpful with the Corby work. We don't squabble. We do laugh a lot because we truly enjoy each other.

She has published a second book and is working on a third. Her special genius is describing people and events in striking detail. Her first book has sold more than a thousand copies in its first year. Not very many self-published books do as well as that.

I tell all of this because it seems like too many people who are alone at age 60 think that love won't or can't happen to them again at their age. My story says it can...and does.

We know we are in the fall of our time together. We don't talk much about death, not that either of us is afraid of it for ourselves, but because we know we still have family events that we want to attend. I want to see Emily succeed, Trevor to have a good place in life, Jer and Josh , their wonderful wives and children grow together in their already happy and meaningful lives. But we all will deal with whatever happens because fear cannot enter our place if we won't let it.

There is a certain pacific benefit that comes with age. Maybe it is an expanding tolerance, or the wisdom to know that some things, many things are just not worth the pain of arguing. By now we know our limits and limitations. By now we treasure our gifts and how they came to be.

Time does take on a new meaning, but we can't stop it or live in its shadowy past. Nimbi's story is now part of mine and vice versa; her heart is part of mine and vice versa. I am grateful for every day with her. Love can happen in the fall. My beauty of autumn is named Nimbi.

—16—

A Gallery of Loved Ones

I have crossed paths with thousands of people in my lifetime. Some have impacted me so deeply that I need to say a few words about them.

Space limitations limit this gallery to my immediate family and best friend. To all the others who could have been cited, I thank you every day.

Jeremy Langford

Though Jeremy and Josh are very different in many ways, the fact that their parents were divorced brought them together in a bond that is unbreakable. Except for their spouses, they are each other's best friend.

Jeremy has some of the traits I like to claim for myself. He is a writer, a reader, an editor, a public speaker, and he is passionate in his loyalties. Outgoing and with a gift for imitation and humor, he makes friends easily and more than superficially. But our similarities surrender there; he is organized, orderly, neat, carefully precise, and he never uses bad language.

While still in grade school, Jeremy and Josh came to live with Jill and me in the house we had recently purchased on Erskine Boulevard in South Bend. It was not an easy transition but we all did what we could to make it work. Jeremy is two years older than Josh, so he was the first to need a decision about where to go to high school. We could have sent him to St. Joseph High School, where I had gone, but I felt that it had become important in contemporary life to be exposed to diversity with all of its benefits and potential pitfalls. So Jeremy and Josh both went to Riley High School, just down the street from where we lived. It was a good experience for them. They came under the influence of some very good teachers, made lasting friendships, took advanced placement courses and participated in varsity tennis and baseball. In addition, both were excellent at hockey and played in a league hosted at Notre Dame.

While they were still at Riley, we knew we needed a larger house and we found a wonderful home on East Fairview St. I enlarged the facility by having a builder construct an apartment in the basement for the boys. They loved it. I'm not sure what nefarious adventures were launched there, (and I don't want to know), but all in all, it was a good arrangement.

We were all delighted when Jeremy received his acceptance letter from Notre Dame. He would be the third generation of Langfords to study there. We budgeted so he, and in two years his brother too, could live on campus and share the full college life. Because I was on the faculty, their tuition, if the child could earn acceptance, was gratis, a benefit that was also extended to staff members who had been employed by the University for at least ten years. What an incredible benefit!

Jeremy's four years at Notre Dame were outstanding. He liked reading, studying, living in Sorin Hall, his many friends, and his proximity to home. His double major in English and Philosophy fit him perfectly.

While an editor at Loyola Press, 1993-1997, Jeremy had a once-in-a-lifetime experience. The much-beloved Cardinal of Chicago, Joseph Bernardin, was suffering with cancer and the prognosis was not hopeful. The Cardinal wanted to write a final book to leave as part of his legacy. Jeremy signed the project for Loyola Press, where he then was in charge of acquisitions and he began to visit the Cardinal regularly to go over the manuscript as it developed. They worked diligently together. Jeremy was able to present proofs of the book to the Cardinal shortly before he died.

The book, *The Gift of Peace: Personal Reflections* by Joseph Cardinal Bernardin, went on to make the *New York Times* bestseller list.

The Cardinal died on November 14, 1996. For the next four years, Jeremy and Fr. Alphonse Spilly, C.PP.S. worked together to gather the best of the Cardinal's writings, sermons and reflections. They were co-editors of Cardinal Bernardin's book, *The Journey to Peace: Reflections on Faith, Embracing Suffering and Finding New Life.*

In 1997, Jeremy accepted the position of Executive Editor of Sheed and Ward and moved with it when it was purchased by Rowman and Littlefield. In 2005, he became Director of Communications for the Chicago Province of the Jesuits (now the Midwest Province). He is chair of the communications committee for the Jesuits in the U.S. and Canada as well as being on the advisory board for the Jesuit Curia in Rome. In other words, he is a communications leader. His skills also show in the books he has written: *God Moments: Why Faith Really Matters to a New Generation* (Orbis 2001) and *Seeds of Faith: Practices to Grow a Healthy Spiritual Life* (Paraclete 2007) He has co-edited and contributed to other books as well. His books have been widely and favorably received. My favorite review of his first book says this:

"...Langford's is a humble, authentic, and intellectual voice that readers of all ages and faith traditions will appreciate." — *Publishers Weekly* (Starred Review 11/16/01).

I've enjoyed many wonderful times with Jeremy, but my favorite was the several days we spent together in New York City. We were there to see Trace Murphy, an editor at Doubleday, and to negotiate a contract for *The Spirit of Notre Dame* book. We enjoyed our time together and it was nice being free to do so. He took me to meet and hang out with Fr. Dan Berrigan, SJ. Fr. Dan had been a staunch opponent of our involvement in Vietnam. He was on the side of the troops but decidedly not the side of Richard Nixon.

While we were visiting his apartment, I had to use his bathroom. As I sat on the toilet, I noticed a framed document on the wall, eye level, so easily readable. I read it. The document was from the Nixon papers and recorded a meeting Nixon had with his chief advisor, John Erlichman.

They were discussing who were the most dangerous leaders of the anti-war movement. Nixon asked who was the worst. Erlichman replied Dan Berrigan. Nixon said, '"Get him!"

Upon returning to the living room, I asked Fr. Dan why he had that document hanging next to the toilet. He answered, "I like to respond to it every day."

Those days in New York are a treasury of good memories.

Jeremy and Liz are remarkable parents to their three children, Tyler, Caitlin and Colin. Every minute that they can they are encouraging the children to enjoy and grow with every venture they undertake.

Josh Langford

Josh is eighteen months younger than Jeremy. Though they are as close as twins, they are distinctly different personalities. Josh is a bit more laid back and approachable. His smile, which I call the, "Joker Smile" is in a class by itself. Like Jeremy, he has athletic skills in tennis, baseball and hockey.

I never worried about Jeremy in college, but I did worry about Josh. He was smart enough to get along without the same amount of studying that most students have to do. When I expressed my concerns to Professor Jim McAdams, he advised me to relax and said that when Josh finds something that he really wants to do, he will be highly successful.

Somewhere along the way, he developed an ability to set a goal and reach it. When he was a junior at Notre Dame, Josh decided to train for a boxing tournament at Notre Dame, the Bengal Bouts. This is a once-a-year tournament for 240 or so Notre Dame students who are willing to fight in all weight divisions to earn gate receipts for the Holy Cross Missions in Bangladesh. Proceeds from ticket sales exceed $100,000 a year.

Josh went through the rigorous training, learned the rudiments of boxing, and got ready for his first battle. His family and lots of friends showed up to cheer him on. The bouts are a perfect imitation of the old championship fights that used to be broadcast on Friday nights. Josh chose "Josh the Janitor" as his fighting name. The idea was that he would mop up his opponent. That's not the way it turned out. The three-round fight might have been long for him, but it seemed endless to me. He took a pounding but kept coming in for more in the hope of landing a K.O. punch. The head of the tourney, and referee, Tom Suddes, was himself a past champion. He said after the fight that he had never seen a Bengal fighter who took the punches Josh did and still kept coming. I know it was the first time I ever understood wrestling fans who would throw chairs and try to get into the ring to help their favorites. Josh's blood was my blood too. I wanted to get in there and help him. But life takes strange turns. Tom Suddes didn't forget the courage and determination of Josh the Janitor. After graduation, his first career job was with the Suddes Group in Dublin, Ohio. He learned many valuable sales, management and business skills there. When he received a good job offer from Enron in Houston, Texas, he was ready for it.

He learned enough at Enron to move on before the fall of that empire. Next he worked at Verizon where he became a Vice President. By then, he was well versed in the whole process of offering online backup services to large corporations like Best Buy. After several years at Verizon, he decided to get in on the ground floor of a new company in the wine country of California. Although the venue was incredibly beautiful, the company was flat. He and his bride moved back to the Chicago area where he opened an office as Midwest Sales Director for Ipsoft Company, headquartered in New York. Josh grew the business in the Midwest quickly and dramatically. Jim McAdams was right: once Josh knew what he wanted to do, look out above. He married a truly magnificent woman, Cathy Wolf, whose dad is a professor at Notre Dame and whose mother is an accomplished artist. Josh and

Cathy had known each other since high school. They now have two beautiful daughters, Sophia and Gisele, and they live in Northfield, Illinois.

I am very proud of Josh. His professional skills and dedication are most impressive and his personality and dedication to Cathy and the girls even more so.

There is a quality of generosity in Josh that sometimes stuns me. He donates to good causes, supports scholarships at the Cristo Rey school in Chicago, and helps others without seeking any return. But that quality never stunned me more than in 2007 when he called to ask where in the world I'd like to go for ten days as a gift for my 70th birthday. In my heart I had always wished to bring a copy of my Galileo book to his tomb in Florence as a sign of my respect and gratitude. So I said Italy and, if we have time, Normandy.

It turned out that Jeremy couldn't come with us. Although we would miss his company and knowledge of Rome, Josh wanted to go ahead with the trip as his gift. So he made the plans and reservations. On September 6, 2007 our adventure began. It was my first transoceanic flight and I marveled to myself how amazing it is that an airplane could fly that distance, high above the sea below, with not even a hint of danger.

Recently, when I told Josh that I was going to write about our trip for this book, he said that he had kept a journal of it and that he'd send it to me. Reading it brought me back to one of the best weeks of my life. He said I could cite his journal, so here are some excerpts:

Dad and I are similar in our travel and planning habits. Neither of us has an interest in excessive planning or detailed agendas. For this trip, we had what we needed: a flight to Rome, lodging in Rome and Florence, and nine days of unscheduled time to wander freely around Italy.

We took the fast train from Rome to Florence and I was totally taken by the beauty of the Tuscany countryside. If there is reincarnation, I want to come back as a Tuscan grape farmer!

It is impossible not to fall in love with Florence. Once settled in our hotel, we set about to explore the city. We arrived too late to gain admission to Santa Croce, where Galileo is entombed; that would have to wait until tomorrow.

We stopped at the hotel bar for a drink. We sat outside and ended up talking until about 3 a.m., then slept until 11 a.m. We had about five hours to accomplish our tasks. We took a route that brought us straight past the dome of the Florence Cathedral, the first octagonal dome ever built without a temporary wooden support frame. Twenty minutes later we arrived at the church, Santa Croce, which holds the earthly remains of Galileo, Michelangelo, Machiavelli, and Gentile, among others.

Galileo's tomb is in the back right corner; there was a bed of candles in front of it and a guard standing nearby. I gave dad a euro and told him to light a candle for his hero. He said earlier that all he needed was about ten minutes alone with him to pay his respects and say a few things. He told me he prayed that Galileo's innovative and brave spirit would always be alive in the world.

This was the part of the trip dad had anticipated. This moment was worth the journey. To me, this was the 70th birthday present to dad and all the rest was just fun. Dad did as promised and spent only a few minutes with his mentor. He is a precise thinker and concise communicator, I could tell it was all he needed.

One thing Josh did not notice was that I had brought a copy of my book, *Galileo, Science and The Church.* I asked the guard if he would place it at the foot of the sculpture that stood atop the tomb. He was kind enough to do so. I felt like my pilgrimage, my homage, my debt of gratitude to the man I had spent years studying and writing about was now complete.

Josh and I had bonded in seeing all the sites together, having delightful conversation for hours every day over food and wine or walking and observing. Rome was too much to take in—the Coliseum, the Vatican, Sistine Chapel, Pantheon, Mussolini's balcony,the Spanish steps, Piazza Navona, it would take months even to begin to explore, but we relished the days we spent trying to do so.

And the nights were memorable as well. Every night in the Campo di Fiori there was a party, overseen by the statue of Giordano Bruno, that lasted from the first hint of darkness until four or so in the morning. We normally stayed until about three o'clock having food and wine and Guinness or Beamish stout. We never tired of people watching, or topics to discuss. Bruno was a maverick Dominican who was burned at the stake in 1600 for alleged heresy. I felt comfortable celebrating in his statuary presence.

In fact, we never got tired of each other either. Back at the apartment we would sleep until noon and then get some food and continue our sightseeing.

Far too quickly, it was September 15, our departure date for going home. We said goodbye to Giordano Bruno and all the wonders we had seen in Rome and Florence. The trip was the best gift I have ever been given. Josh's touching account of our visit to Galileo's tomb was right, except for his saying it was the single greatest highlight of the trip. For me, it was a tie between Galileo and Josh. What father would not relish every moment, every conversation enjoyed over nine days with his son against a backdrop as fascinating as Rome and Florence? I wish I had taken my dad on a similar trip.

Trevor Langford

Trevor is now 24 years old; he was two before we started noticing that he was unable to speak intelligibly and his coordination was sub-normal. He seemed always to be happy and his comprehension and memory were clearly intact. He has always been, and still is, easy to love. We tried every form of speech therapy and physical exercises with less than the hoped-for results.

Despite his speech and coordination issues, Trev worked his way through LaVille Elementary and LaVille Junior and Senior High School. He was in special education classes and some wonderful teachers worked closely with him and us. It was a proud moment when he earned his class ring and a diploma. It has never depressed him that he is missing some things that most of the people his age experience along the way.

But on his own, he decided to follow in the footsteps of his godfather, Chris Zorich, an All-American tackle for Notre Dame and then the Chicago Bears. When the call went out for signups for varsity football, Trevor answered. During the summer, he showed up for every conditioning session. The coaches were impressed with his determination and grit. They kept him on the team and assigned him number 70. Local columnist Al Lesar heard the story of how he got to play in a regular season game and he wrote this account:

August 31, 2007 | By AL LESAR South Bend Tribune Columnist

LAKEVILLE—Limitations don't define Trevor Langford's life. Prayer and football and maybe a little dancing are better indicators. A 5-foot-10, 235-pound package of "want to" is the heart and soul of the LaVille High School football team, even though he's never played the game before.

The junior special ed student is truly special.

"Everyone out here is his big brother," LaVille coach Brian Stultz said. "Each guy is looking out for him. Trevor means a lot to all of us."

Football means the world to Trevor. Last Thursday night, Aug. 23, before the Lancers scheduled season-opener at Lake Station, he knelt down beside his mom's bed and prayed.

"He said, 'Dear God, please let me play in the game tomorrow,'" Jill Langford said in an e-mail to the LaVille coaches.

Trevor did get to play, though the game was delayed

until Saturday because of the weather. After getting a comfortable lead, Stultz said he called a timeout, informed the Lake Station coach and officials of what he was doing, and sent Trevor into the game with a "buddy."

"We put him at twins (receivers)," Stultz said. "I told him to move when (his buddy) moves, then go after No. 42." "You shoulda seen (No. 42)," teammate Aaron Bettcher said with a laugh. "His eyes got big like, 'Hey, what do I do?' The crowd went crazy. You should've seen the grin on Trevor's face."

Stultz smiled. Teammates Bettcher, Jon Wicks and Doug Spencer all savored the moment.

The whole Lancer team got another chance to enjoy the experience. Before practice Monday, during the film session, Stultz showed the play three times. "I looked over. Trevor had this big ol' grin on his face," Bettcher said. "You knew he loved it."

"Seeing Trevor get in was the highlight of our game," Wicks said. "It was awesome. It was so emotional for the crowd."

"Now I know how to tackle better," Trevor said of what he learned from the film.

"We see him as 'Radio,'" Spencer said, referring to the football movie of the same name. "Watching him go out on the field, he was stiff as stone. Then, when he knew where he was supposed to go, he got all riled up.

"We don't see him as different. We see him as our brother. Looking at Trevor, watching how badly he wants to play makes us play harder." "I love playing football," Trevor said. "My godfather (Chris Zorich) played football (at Notre Dame and the Chicago Bears). Nose guard."

Trevor started pestering Stultz about playing last

year during a computer class. Stultz didn't know what to think. But when Trevor showed up for most of the summer conditioning sessions and two-a-day practices, Stultz knew he was serious.

"Originally, we thought he'd just be an honorary captain," Stultz said. "But he kept showing so much interest and 'want' that we had to give him a shot. We make sure he doesn't get involved into too much contact, but just being a part of this team is something he loves."

"We always have to help him get his (practice) jersey on 'cause it's so tight," Wicks said. Even though it doesn't fit, Trevor must wear the No. 50 jersey— Zorich's number.

Besides fulfilling his role as one of several captains, walking to midfield before the game for the coin flip, Trevor has another significant duty on the team. "After every practice, Trevor sets his pads down, puts his head down and cranks up the stereo," Wicks said. "He's a big AC/DC guy."

"He can come up with some pretty wild dances," Bettcher said. "Trevor starts going and everyone starts dancin.'"

No limits spoil his fun."

Trevor Langford will never go to college, probably never get married, likely will not hold a significant job, but he will always bring joy, happiness and true friendship to all who know him. In his own way, he is a hero. If sometimes we need to be reminded how fortunate we are to be running on all cylinders, people like Trevor are there to teach us, challenge us, by showing that it doesn't matter what hand you are dealt in life.

What matters is how well you play the hand you were dealt. Score 100% for Trevor.

Emily Alice Langford

All dads are proud of their daughters. I am no exception. Even though she has done some things and made some decisions that I truly wish she hadn't, the good in her has always shined brightly enough to eclipse these differences.

Emily was three days old when we brought her home from the South Bend Osteopathic Hospital where she was born. She is biracial and has grown into a lovely young lady. Don't ask me why, but once I was tuned in to the physical characteristics of biracial people, I have realized how attractive so many of the blended population are.

Even though she attended a rural Midwest school, her schoolmates readily accepted and befriended her. In fact, her fourth-grade class at LaVille Elementary raised enough money to buy ten bicycles to donate to There Are Children Here. Some parents had reservations about this since the camp was for inner-city children. But the LaVille students had no reservations at all. Would that their attitude could reach out across the whole country.

Emily played on the soccer and basketball teams in grade school and became a track star in high school, winning numerous medals and ribbons. And she took up playing trumpet in the LaVille band.

I will never forget the courage she showed on an extraordinary occasion. One of the books I guided to publication at Rowman and Littlefield was a collection of meditations that were presented over the years at the Rockefeller Chapel of the University of Chicago surrounding or punctuating the performance by the Vermeer String Quartet of Franz Joseph Haydn's *The Seven Last Words of Christ*. The radio broadcast note declared it:

> During Holy Week, Rockefeller Memorial Chapel will present a special performance of Franz Joseph Haydn's *The Seven Last Words of Christ*, an annual musical production by the world-renowned Vermeer String Quartet, at 8 p.m. Wednesday, April 11. Eight distinguished theologians will accompany the quartet's performance with their original meditations on the last words of Jesus Christ.

The performance year in and year out was a revered tradition and the invited speakers over the years read like a who's who of American theology, including people like Rev. Martin Luther King, Barack Obama, Martin Marty, Andrew Greeley, Jean Bethke Elshtain, Alison Boden, Billy Graham and Raymond Brown. Because of my work with There Are Children Here, I was invited to offer a meditation on the passage "My God, My God. Why have you forsaken me?" I chose to speak on behalf of the children at There Are Children Here who, all too often, knew what the feeling of abandonment is. I asked Richard Young whether Emily could read my meditation from the pulpit. He said, "Of course."

Emily was, and to some extent still is, somewhat shy. She practiced the reading for days before the event. But, sitting next to me in the choir stalls as speakers gave eloquent deliveries, her little heart began to tell her to have me do it in her stead. Her eyes began to tear up. I assured her that it was all right and that I'd read it for her. When our turn came, she looked at me, and said she would do it. That took genuine courage and character. She delivered it well, so well that in the reception held afterward, she was the speaker most congratulated.

Though never really outgoing, she was well liked at school and by our friends. Though never an academic whiz, she did well enough to gain acceptance to Holy Cross College, Notre Dame, Indiana. Her four years there were good for her. At the end of her senior year, she delivered a capstone presentation on her life with ease and grace. It took me back to that pulpit at Rockefeller Chapel.

During her four years at Holy Cross College, Emily was a member of the highly regarded Notre Dame Marching Band. She traveled with the band to away games in both football and basketball and that gave her a chance to experience locales all over the country. I kidded Jeremy and Josh that there was finally a Langford on the field on a football Saturday at Notre Dame. The friendships she made with band members will be with her all her life. All her mother and I wish for her is what every parent does for their children: happiness in this life with eternal joy to follow.

Lois and Bill

My older sister, Lois was always a bright student, a hard worker, a help to our mother and far too organized to be on my wave length. The five year age gap between us meant that we didn't get to share much growing up. She entered college when I was still in eighth grade. She was different enough from us that my brother and I tried unsuccessfully to convince her that she was adopted.

I took an interest in her dating life mainly because one of her boyfriends had a Cushman motor scooter and another was a boxer in the Bengal Bouts tournament at Notre Dame. But eventually she hit the jackpot; she met and dated Bill Berry, a Notre Dame Electrical Engineering student from Shelby, Ohio. After graduation they were married. Bill went on to earn his masters and doctorate degrees and came back to join the faculty at Notre Dame. Lois was a teacher at a Catholic grade school in South Bend; they settled in a lovely home in the Harter Heights neighborhood in South Bend and had four children: Elizabeth, Bill, Suzanne and Tom, all of whom excelled in their academic pursuits. They all turned out to be wonderful people.

Lois and Bill are among the best, kindest and most accomplished people I've ever known. I say that in spite of the fact that Bill never had a Cushman or competed in boxing, and Lois far too often impinged on my third of the backseat on our marathon drives from South Bend to Mexico City and back.

Walter and Barbara

My brother, Walter, is nearly four years my senior. Though very different in looks and personality, we had a tacit but real closeness over the years. He graduated from Notre Dame in 1955 and, having been in the Air Force ROTC, he was commissioned a lieutenant in the Air Force and reported to Lackland Air Force Base near San Antonio, Texas, to begin his training. He made a career in the Air Force including Air-Sea Rescue in Japan and active duty in Vietnam. He retired as a Lt. Colonel, and worked for the State of California. His and Barbara's blended family include Jim, Sarah, Tom and Kathi, Roger, Wendy and Julie.

Barbara has been diagnosed with dementia and early-onset Alzheimers and Walter, with help from the children who live in California, have shown their unwavering love in how they care for her. He is a hero in my book.

Walter and Barb were there when I needed them and I hold them close in my heart.

Libby and John

Liz (now Libby) was born 11 years after I was. She was a surprise. Mom used to refer to her as "My autumn lamb." She was that and more. Everybody loved her and we all combined to spoil her. She was cute, quick and happy. None of her much older siblings really got to know her well. But we were all happy for her when she had the experience of a lifetime. At the age of 13, she went to Chile with our mom and dad and the Peace Corps volunteers in dad's group. Those two years taught her a lot about discovering a wonderful culture, expanding her worldview and joining people who devote part of their lives to helping the less fortunate.

She is a graduate of St. Mary's College and eventually became an administrator in a med-tech operation. She and her husband, John, have lived for years in New Jersey. John beat cancer, sold his appliance store in Staten Island, and shares in the work of breeding and raising championship AKC dogs. We don't see each other as often as we should, but we love each other and that's as it should be.

Dad

When I was growing up, I idolized and respected my dad, but I didn't get to know him as well as I would have liked. He brought an enormous amount of good into the world as a teacher, coach, Peace Corps director, and tireless worker for good causes. His example of dedication and zeal motivated me and likely contributed to my later inability to tolerate mediocrity and indifference.

In researching for my book *Quotable Notre Dame*, I came across a story, told by a 1947 walk-on tennis player, Phil Lyons, that illustrates the kind of person he was.

> When the final meet of the season rolled around I needed just one more victory to earn my monogram, but I had just about abandoned any hope of getting that coveted award, because the road trip limit was

seven or eight players and I had very little chance of ousting anyone from the road roster.

...Out of nowhere, Coach Langford told me to pack my gear for the trip...I was inserted into the number six singles spot by Langford, who in turn proceeded to divide his attention among all six singles matches.

Every time the coach glanced my way, I was struggling. But I was winning the big points. It was a hard fought match and I won. I felt great because I had won my monogram.

After the match, Coach Langford came up to me and said he was going to enter me in the number three doubles with Bill Tully because with Bill as my partner, I was guaranteed a win and a monogram.

When I told him I had won my singles match, he was just about flabbergasted. He smiled, congratulated me, and went back to his regular doubles team.

I'll never forget his love for his players or the players' love for Coach Langford.

Growing up I heard over and over from his players, his students and the Peace Corps volunteers how they regarded him as their "second father." It made me a little jealous; I wish I had known him better.

I think my most memorable moment with him was in 1961. He was in Washington, D.C. for a Peace Corps meeting and I was there doing research at the Library of Congress for my Galileo book. We spent the better part of an afternoon talking, sitting on the famous Bernard Baruch's bench in Lafayette Park.

As he grew into his late eighties, he began to suffer from dementia and then from full-blown Alzheimers which claimed his life at the age of 92. My brother and

I visited him in the assisted-living place that was caring for him. It broke my heart when asked me: "When did we meet?" But he made my heart sing when he then said, "You seem like a very nice man."

I said back to him, "You are a very nice man." He truly was.

Mom

Even though we were too similar to be best friends, this little dynamo of a woman marked me forever. She helped me grow up through the years I was bullied, the years I managed some maturity in high school, and the years I spent in the Dominicans. Even though I know it broke her heart when I left the priesthood, she was sensitive to me that summer at home and it was her advice that made my mind up to seek my new life in New York. She was our main parent as we grew up. Hardworking, ever active, always generous and a wonderful cook, she was the glue in our family.

I have many warm memories of her, throughout my childhood. I will always cherish her tears that day at the age of 11 when I came out from physical therapy walking in an almost limp-free way. But I think the memory that stays with me most vividly happened when I visited my parents at La Romana in the Dominican Republic.

In real time it was a discussion over a few hours while walking on the beach and climbing large rocks to get a better view of the ocean.. I got to know her heart that day and learned how she looked back on her life. I can still see her, not as she looked on her deathbed, but with all the vitality that she patented through her life and on that beach. I hope one day in the next world to resume our talk and to partake, metaphorically, in one of her unforgettable meals. Food always tastes better when it is cooked with love.

Mr. Resilience: Tim Carroll

I have known Tim Carroll for some 40 years. I first met him when he owned and operated Regency Typographics, a company that set type in hot metal, a process that embodied elegance and quality. He would come to Notre Dame Press to sell us on hot metal for our books and advertising pieces. His business suffered when publishers turned to computers to prepare pages for the printer. Tim grew up in the printing business; his dad owned a number of suburban newspapers in the Chicago area. Tim knew well the smell of ink as it takes to paper.

Even back then I thought that Tim was an interesting guy. He was very knowledgeable, always helpfully amiable and, one could tell, an interesting character. As I came to know him over time, I learned just how interesting! His life is a story that would take a book to tell. His ups and downs and ups again are legendary.

When hot metal type was no longer used, the new methods being less expensive, Tim became a print broker who matched publishers with the best printing company for their projects. He traveled extensively and his Irish friendliness made him many friends among publishers and printers.

Later, he was plant manager of the printing operation at Ave Maria Press at Notre Dame. Subsequently he founded a company, Championship Programs, which prepares and prints annual programs for state trapshooting associations around the country. He is, himself, an excellent trapshooter and an avid duck hunter. Most of all he is a good friend. I count him as my best male friend.

I don't have the right or space to tell many Tim stories, but here are a few that will create anticipation for a full biography someday.

Tim and a friend were traveling in the friend's big and expensive RV to a trapshooting tourney. As they approached the locale, Tim said that his friend should take over the driving in order to park it safely in the campgrounds space. His friend said, "No, you can do it." Bad mistake. He did manage to back it into a tight space between two other RVs, but then he hit the button to expand the sides outward. One side crashed into the RV on his right. He got out to survey the damage, meet the owners of the damaged vehicle and he invited them in for a martini or two and ended up with new friends. Up and down and up again.

Then there is the tale of how he won $5,000 in the lottery and decided to take a trip in the small, used RV he had recently purchased. He filled it with gas and drove to the credit union to get some cash. The credit union had just re-paved its entire parking lot. Tim pulled up and parked. When he came out of the credit union, he was horrified to discover that his full tank of gas was now flowing over the parking lot. The tank, thanks to a 97-cent part, had leaked its contents. HazMat had to be called to clean it up. Some of the new asphalt would have to be replaced. He would soon get a bill for for close to the $5,000 he had won in the lottery.

He replaced the part, filled it with gas and was off on his trip.

Up and down and up again.

More recently, he had delicate eye surgery at Northwestern Hospital in Chicago. In a few days, it was beginning to heal. It was cold so he built a fire in his fireplace and lay down in front of it. He fell asleep. His dog came up to him and, sensing that he had a wound, licked his eye. It got infected. He needed to get the whole operation re-done. Up and down and up again.

Tim is the story of Job told in modern terms. Remember how that story turned out? Up and down but always up again. I am proud to have Tim as a close friend and colleague.

And the Many Others
Who Have Impacted My life

Each of us could spend hours and days recalling names and faces from our past in an effort to chart those who, momentarily or permanently, have impacted our life. Friends, teachers, coaches, employers, advisers, priests, nuns and brothers, colleagues, and so on. It is a good idea to do that because it serves to remind us that we have not gone through life as an island; we are part of something bigger, something more than chance and circumstance. I wish I could list here all of the people who, knowingly or not, made an impression that now flows through my memory like an endless, non-stop slide show. It would take too long to list or catalog them. Whether we like it or not, we are all part of the human race; we are part of each other. The implications of that truth, if we would let them, could radically change how we view each other, regardless of skin color, culture, status or beliefs. This is not to say that all things are relative, but it is to say that all things are related.

It is a truth that what Catholic doctrine calls the Mystical Body of Christ is real. John Donne was right: "Ask not for whom the bell tolls, it tolls for thee." When I respond on Facebook to someone's post about the death of a relative or friend I do not say, "I'm sorry for your loss." My response is, I am sorry for our loss." And I mean it.

—17—

Of Regrets and Surprises

W ho of us, after living a whole life, can look back with no regrets? Hindsight seems always to hold a better hand than actual history does.

Of course were we to go back, knowing what we know now, and change things, make different decisions, right the wrongs, maybe we could somehow emerge as the person we always wanted to be. But we don't have a flex capacitor at our disposal. It is what it was. There can be no revising or forging the record.

When I was growing up, the nuns taught us that God knows everything we do. Mix that with Judgment Day and you begin to see God as some kind of scorekeeper or heavenly accountant, filling a ledger with credits and debits that will cause God metaphorically to move His thumb up or down, thus determining our eternal fate. We were told to love God but not taught exactly how to do that. God was ethereal, all-knowing, all-seeing and all-hiding too. The catechism taught a simplified version that often tended to build faith in an unseen being who was fair but kind. But then so was Santa Claus.

With time and the trials of growing up, the picture of God changed somewhat. Faith was given flesh and bones in the person of Jesus, His apostles and saints. Much was made of the Stations of the Cross and Good Friday. Jesus suffered and died for our sins and thereby established a new bond between God and the human race. Less was made, back then, of Easter Sunday and the conquering of death itself. Even if I didn't always live it, I did believe it.

In high school, the pragmatic demands of coming of age, wishing for identity, acceptance, independence and some manner of dealing with the widening of the gap between prohibited behavior and the powerful urges of blossoming sexuality, made it seem that religion was more about what not to do than it was about the positive actions that belief could inspire. Still, I did not cancel my beliefs even if I often failed to act on them. In my heart of hearts, I counted on God's mercy more than on His justice.

In my year at Notre Dame it began to come together for me in a more cogent way. God seemed more real and closer on that campus and in a real theology classroom. My professor was Fr. Fred Barr, CSC and his gift to the class was not only his clear and rational presentation of Catholic theology, but also the gentle goodness of his life. He counseled me about my interest in the priesthood and never undersold or oversold the rigors and blessings of that vocation. Every time I visit the Holy Cross Community Cemetery on campus, I stop at his grave and thank him for his guidance.

As I progressed through eight years of intensive study and prayer, I was eager to learn everything I could from the disciplines of philosophy, scripture, theology and history. It all fit for me; I saw the logic, the congruence, the all-inclusive worldview that made Catholicism vital for me. I studied deeply and learned well and, in the process, my faith grew.

Though faith is a gift, the admonition of St. James is its proviso: "For the body without the spirit is dead, so faith without works is dead also." From the first days of my ministry to the last days of my life, the "works" that faith requires are the beatitudes, the incarnations of love, that come from faith and lead back to its deepening. This became more than a conviction; it became my focus to the point where my very soul seemed to be engraved with the warning in the Book of Revelations 3:15-16: "I know your works: you are neither hot nor cold. Would that you were either cold or hot! So because you are lukewarm and neither hot nor cold, I will spit you out of my mouth." Tough words. But if you have put everything on the line to follow the Lord, they are words that need to be heard and heeded.

My literal understanding of those words led me to be univocal in their application to those I lived with at Holy Rosary in Minneapolis. In retrospect who was I to judge them? For all I know, they might have been holier than I would ever be, even if their holiness was immanent rather than transient, interior rather than visible in action. I owe them an apology for my pride.

After I asked to be released from the priesthood, I could have simply said goodbye to the Church. I didn't, even after attending Mass at a parish in Kew Gardens where the priest gave a sermon on the topic of priests who were leaving the priesthood. He said we are like Judas and doing the work of Satan. Of course I wanted to stand up and challenge him. Instead I sat there. The next thing I knew, the ushers were coming by with collection baskets. I had a ballpoint pen and a grocery receipt on me. I wrote the good padre a note and put it in the basket. What it said is known only to God, that priest and me. I suppose some who are reading this could make a guess or two about the message conveyed.

My prayer life over the past couple of decades has been much more regular than my church attendance has been. I have no explanation or excuse for that. I try to live a good life, to practice the beatitudes, to provide donations, clothes, food and encouragement to causes that touch my heart.

The nearly 17 years at There Are Children Here have to stand as my spiritual bouquet. The memory of those days and weeks, months and years, and the faces, smiles and inspiration they brought into my life, live in me now and will to my last moment on earth. Those, not even the seminary and priesthood, are my deepest ties to spiritual meaning and growth. They were built and buttressed by the cheerful grace the Notre Dame students brought to the place and the children. My neighbor, Elson Fish was right when he said this is what Jesus would do. When someone tells me that he or she doubts that God exists, my answer is that I know He does; I've met His children.

Notre Dame has always been a touchstone for my belief. My soul has been nurtured there. I need only to walk on that campus to feel grace. It is hard to love, really love, an abstract God, but it is not hard to love God in the Holy Family. The Virgin Mary stands atop this place, crushing the snake under her feet and just feet away the statue of Jesus with outstretched arms reaches out to those walking by. There has been and is more good in this place than in any place I have ever been.

Grace is a gratuitous gift from God. It is promised through the sacraments, and they serve to highlight it. But it is also there for the asking in non-sacramental ways. It is grace that inspires us and lifts us. Douglas Coupland put it beautifully:

> Here is my secret: I tell it to you with an openness of heart that I doubt I shall ever achieve again, so I pray you are in a quiet room as you hear these words. My secret is that I need God—that I am sick and can no longer make it alone. I need God to help me give,

because I no longer seem capable of giving; to help me be kind, as I no longer seem capable of kindness; to help me love, as I seem beyond being able to love.

St. Thomas argued that human nature itself is basically good. Grace does not replace human nature, it simply calls out the best in us and supplies human nature with the will and strength to reach its fulfillment. Rabbi Abraham Heschel said it perfectly:

> A religious person is a person who holds God and humanity in one thought at one time, at all times, who suffers harm done to others, whose greatest passion is compassion, whose greatest strength is love and defiance of despair.

As I look back over my life, my main regret is that I failed to thank personally some of the people to whom I owed gratitude but neglected to pay. We all have people, some recognized and remembered, some not, who helped form us into the person we are now, virtues and faults included. The stories of us all are woven into a cloth only God can see and admire. God is present, ready to come to our aid—even when we forget to summon Him.

Of course, I am appalled by some of the things I've done or not done along the way. I agree with Maya Angelou: "We may encounter many defeats but we must not be defeated." Since this book is not titled *Confessions*, I won't go into any detail.

In my life there were more than enough promises to go around: I broke my promise to be a priest forever.

Religious life broke its promise to provide a community of like-minded brothers who dedicated their lives to serve God with zeal and generosity. The Church, through its administrators, broke its promise to allow enough freedom to probe for the truth. I broke my promise to be there for not one, but two wives. This terrible independence of mine; I don't know how far back it goes. Might it have come from self awareness? Or from living with a defective left side? All I know is that the one promise I never broke was to love and nurture all who came to There Are Children Here. As for everyone else who I encountered along the way and through the years, to those I have affected adversely, I ask forgiveness. To those I failed to help when they needed me, I ask for an opportunity to make it up to them.

To those brave enough to love me, my every breath says thank you. I need you to know that even though I could not publish here the list that has your name on it, you are engraved in my memory and my heart.

I hope to live more years with my Nimbi. It took a lifetime to find her and we both pray that our autumn love can display its beauty for years to come.

I am not afraid of dying. But I hope death arrives in the night and that what leads up to it will not be a burden to those I love. For me, the "other side" means meeting my mom and dad again, and other family members whom I never met in person. I know my mom and dad and Leroy Rouner will be there to welcome me and Mary T. Dempsey too. And what a grand reunion it will be to once more enjoy my friends from childhood, high school, the Dominicans, my bosses in publishing, authors, camp volunteers, and the teachers who gave me so much inspiration all along the way. To you who have read this book, I wish every happiness.

Let me say one more time: In the long run, what really matters is who and what you loved, the example you set for others, the way you accepted the good and the not good in your life. And, above all, the grace that God sent through you to those who needed your embrace, your words, your inspiration and your love.